GETTING A GRIP ON
Time Management

*Tools and tips on how to do goal setting,
prioritise, be more efficient and
still have work life balance*

Fully Revised Second Edition

ROBYN PEARCE

getting
agrip
publishing

getting
agrip
publishing

Published by Getting a Grip Publishing, 25 Keven Road,
R.D. 4, Pukekohe 2679, New Zealand

The author asserts her moral rights in the work.
A catalogue record for this book is available from the
National Library of New Zealand

ISBN 978-0-9582460-8-8 – KDP
ISBN 978-0-9582460-7-1 – eBook & Kindle

First published 1996 as *Getting a Grip on Time* by Reed Publishing (NZ) Ltd
Multiple reprints since 1998
Completely revised 2d edition 2018

Cover design by Jeffrey Goh

Printed via KDP

Disclaimer

Legislation, regulations, conditions and governing
authorities vary from country to country.
While the best possible care has been taken in researching and presenting
this material, practises vary in different countries and from year to year.
The author and publisher take no responsibility for the operation of your
application of any suggestions contained in this book.

Also by Robyn Pearce

Books

Getting a Grip on the Paper War
Getting a Grip on Leadership with LaVonn Steiner
About Time –120 time-saving tips for those with no time
About Time for Teaching – 120 time-saving tips
for teachers and those who support them
Getting a Grip on Parenting Time: 86 common sense lessons from the trenches

Books and Reports In digital format only
How to Master Time in Only 90 Seconds - Report
Getting a Grip on Simple Goalsetting
Getting a Grip on Effective Meetings

Other Products
Getting a Grip on Life Goals Toolkit – a workbook
Getting a Grip on Planning and Prioritising – 4-module Online Study Course

To thank you for purchasing this book I also have a very special offer for you.

5 hours and $175 worth of cutting edge information – ALL FREE!!!
Grab the gems from some of the world's top Thought Leaders on Efficiency and Productivity

If you go now to http://gettingagrip.com/digitalgifts **you can download our top five most-requested audios from the 'Getting a Grip on Time' Premier Audio Series**

Dr James Brown – highly awarded ex-NASA project manager and engineer. He shares the techniques he now teaches so that huge projects can be completed on-time and within budget. You'll be surprised how simple and effective yet little-used some of his methods are. For example, when to walk out of meetings, how to chase up tardy colleagues without annoying them, and much more....

Lauren Parsons – wellbeing specialist. Lauren will give you heaps of really simple practical ways to 'snack on exercise'. No longer will you say 'I don't have time to exercise.' She makes it *so* easy.

Mark Sutherland – coach of many Olympic Gold Medallists and now a coach of executives as he interviews me, **Robyn Pearce.** We share tips on how to overcome the 'too much to do and not enough time' syndrome.

Steuart Snooks – one of the world's top information management specialists. You might be surprised at how much time is wasted in today's corporates due to email and other interruptions. Steuart will share with you heaps of tips on how to claw back much of that wasted time, by managing email and excessive information in more efficient ways.

Leo Babauta – hugely successful blogger of Zen Habits, shares his philosophy on goals (you'll be surprised at his perspective), raising children (he's got 6), simplicity ... and much more.

Don't wait – before you start reading, grab your free bonuses at

http://gettingagrip.com/digitalgifts

When you register to get your downloads you'll also receive a well-spaced supply of ongoing time tips and practical help.

Should you wish to unsubscribe at any time,
it's as easy as one click.
We value your commitment to winning your time battles. We don't spam you and *never* share your details.

CONTENTS

DEDICATION

A huge thank you to the wonderful people through the years who've attended my speeches and courses, read my books, articles, ezines and blog and/or listened to my podcasts and then gone out and changed their lives. You inspire me to continue this work.

Also – to all the happy and loyal readers who've said nice things about the first edition of this book and then bought other titles as they arrived. Thank you for sharing your experiences and successes. Your stories have helped those who came after you.

I might be a student of time but it's hard to know where the years since 1996, when the first edition of this book appeared, have gone!

PREFACE TO THE FIRST EDITION (still relevant all these years later!)

If you struggle with getting a grip on your time, run frantically around in circles, and know that if only the day were a bit longer you'd be able to catch up, welcome!

If the people with tidy desks really brass you off, the punctual ones always look smug as you slide red-faced into the room and you hate the look on your boss's face when you have to ask for an extension of time, take heart.

If you've ever been shut out of a meeting because you were too late, missed the chance of important business because you made a bad impression with your lateness, or forgot an urgent deadline because the relevant information was buried under a mountain of paper, hope is around the corner.

If your family constantly comment on your work load, your friends say, *'We never see you these days'* and life seems to be rapidly passing you by, take time to read.

If, with laughter and with anguish, you've ever said *'I just want a life'*, this book is for you.

You have the answers – in your hands. I've been through all the charming experiences above, worked with many others who've specialised in the same delightful habits and the good news is – *there is a better way.*

PREFACE TO THIS SECOND EDITION

It was 1995 and to my delight and surprise Reeds, at the time New Zealand's premier and longest-established publishing house (now taken over, sadly, by a big international conglomerate and split asunder) had said *'we'd like to publish your book'*. I'd sent them a manuscript – putting into it everything I knew about time. At the time I was a fairly new entrant to the time management world and had fallen into it by chance, as you'll read further on.

For a few years I was sure the only reason Reeds had chosen my book was because the senior editor who'd been tasked with considering the manuscript was somewhat challenged with the topic herself! However, kind remarks started to arrive and the readership from around the world expanded, including publication in a number of foreign languages. Within three years of the first edition it became a best-seller in both New Zealand and Australia and it's continued to be reprinted year after year.

'I was told this book is really three books in one. I would almost say it is nearly all the books I've read about time management, goalsetting and effective habits in one. Easy to read and full of practical ideas. Puts a whole new and simple perspective on goalsetting and why the strict focused way blows most of us out of the water' **Elle Anderson, Life Coach.**

'My secretary has been reading **Getting a Grip on Time** *on the bus – keeps coming in to work and quoting bits to me! What we both like, just like your speech, is how easy it is to read and take in, and so very down to earth. It leaves the reader feeling confident that the suggestions are easy to do and motivated to get into action.'* **Denise Bovaird, Past President, New Zealand Institute of Chartered Accountants.**

So what's new in this one?
If you've already got the first edition of *Getting a Grip on Time* and

you're wondering whether to get the update, I think you'll find it worthwhile. This is a significantly different book. Although a few chapters are similar, the first half is very different and the title has been expanded to *Getting a Grip on Time Management*. Over the years I've made major changes to the way I explain the topic, based on 25 years of constantly seeking ways to make the complex simple.

Also, and this is a huge reminder about of how much our world has changed since the 1990s, in the first edition you'll find very few references to computers and no reference to the web or email. One source says that in 1993, a couple of years before my manuscript was handed to the publishers, there were only 130 websites in the whole world and by the end of that year, an MIT researcher counted 623. Even by the time my first 'baby' saw light of day in mid-1996 there were still only a handful of early adopters, academics and military using email. No-one used it commercially as their main method of communication. And even more amazing when we consider essential equipment for any modern office today – even in the late 1990's many people didn't know how to turn a computer on, let alone do the bulk of their work on one.

These days we can't talk about time without dealing with the impact of our digital age – it's changed so much of the way we do our daily business. So in this edition you'll find constant references to computers, email and the web plus a new chapter of my best time-saving email strategies. As with all the other chapters, the new chapter on email will give you a good general coverage and enough practical techniques for immediate improvement.

The main other additions are examples and stories from clients to illustrate key points. Because I now have clients, correspondents and readers of my *Top Time Tips* ezine dotted all round the world, every week brings new stories to add to my repertoire. So, where appropriate you'll find some of those.

What a gift my own previously poor time skills have turned out to be. Thank you, dear readers, for being part of my ever-expanding journey of learning and discovery, constantly seeking for common sense practical answers. Your contributions are always welcome – I learn something from every group or individual I work with.

By the way, in case you're looking at several of my titles and wondering which is the right book for you, each of the *'Getting a grip'* titles gives you a good comprehensive coverage of the topic it addresses. The *'About Time'* series are tips books. (You'll find the full range of my products, in a range of mediums, described at _www.gettingagrip. com_. Soon they will also all be available on Amazon and there are more descriptions at the end of this book.)

PART ONE

WHO'S IN CHARGE OF YOUR SHOW?

How to Kick the Other Guys
Out of Your Driving Seat
and Take Charge of Your Own Life!

CHAPTER 1 SOME BASICS BEFORE WE START

THE BEGINNING OF MY JOURNEY

In the mid-1980s I was a single mother of six children, struggling to survive. My commercial experience was virtually nil. Eventually I ended up in a major city. With my limited business skills and knowledge it was a challenge but an exciting one – a challenge that I grasped with both hands. However, it didn't take me very long to realise that, although I was a very hard worker, one of my greatest weaknesses and limiting behaviours was the way I used my time. Although I got good results it was often at the expense of my health and my personal time.

When, as a burnt-out real estate agent, I heard my first talk on time management, it was like manna from heaven. Finally, here were some simple steps I could take and practical skills I could learn that would help me work smarter, continue to make a good income and at the same time also get some life back. I started reading, studying and practising. It was a shock when people started asking *me* for help – I hadn't realised how much I'd improved until others started knocking at my door. A few years after that first speech I found myself leaving real estate and specialising in helping others with the same time challenges. So, the advice you read in this book has been learnt the hard way – in the trenches. No fancy theories here – all practical road-tested simple-to-apply common sense.

The last 25 years have been a wonderful and exciting journey as an author, keynote speaker and educator. To my amusement, I'm now known around the world as the Time Queen. It's a long way from being always late for everything!

THE LOGIC BEHIND THIS BOOK

A conversation with a young man who'd just finished a three-hour programme with me underpins the way we'll look at this topic. He said: *'I've attended quite a few time management programmes before but yours is different.'*

You guessed it – I asked why.

After a minute's consideration he replied: *'Most courses just tell you what to do. You didn't do that. Instead you gave us the knowledge and space to think about the topic and to make decisions relevant to our own needs.'*

I profoundly believe that there is always more than one 'right way' to achieve great results. Treat the information offered in this book as a delicious buffet – just take what works for you. Rather than having rigid structures and processes thrown at you, you'll unwrap a simple framework and practical explanations to help you make the right decision for yourself at any given moment.

Our most important skill in this digital world is the ability to make rapid decisions, not so much about what to *do* but more about what to *eliminate*. For that we just need a clear decision-making framework, not a whole bunch of rules.

As well as sharing what I know about time management, another major purpose in writing this book is to help you achieve your goals, whatever they may be. (And if you're like about 80 percent of the people on our programmes – not clear on exactly what your goals are – don't worry. We'll address that later.)

WHAT IS THIS THING CALLED TIME MANAGEMENT?

We can't *manage* time. Once we've used this minute, this 30 minutes, it's gone. It's irreplaceable. We can't save it or store it – we can only spend it. *Time* management is a misnomer. We can only manage ourselves; time is just the currency.

Instead, think of it as *energy* management. We *can* manage that, unless we're suffering some serious illness. How do you feel when you're making progress on a key activity or task? And conversely, what happens to your energy levels when you procrastinate on something you know you really ought to be doing? How effective are you when you're really tired? Or unfit? Can you work well or are you just going through the motions? Try using your energy levels as a filter and diagnostic tool and you might be surprised at what you learn about yourself.

We can also manage our expectations, our attitude, our choices of activity. If we fail to do so, then events control us. And when this happens we experience tension, stress, burnout, unhappiness and/or depression.

So, we could also call it *life* management. The tricky thing about life is that it doesn't operate in a nice tidy fashion; instead it's rather like an octopus – multiple elements happening simultaneously and all going in different directions. How do we control these seemingly uncontrollable multiple elements?

KEY POINT No. 1: *When we manage our energy, our choices of activity and our own and other people's expectations, time takes care of itself.*

THE SECRET OF TIME EXCELLENCE

How can we become more effective in the various areas of our lives? What makes a person successful, in whatever way we define success? I believe that *focus* is the key.

There's a very fine line between failing and succeeding. People who fail often work as hard as those who succeed. The major difference is that successful people put their time into activities that give higher pay-back. They're more productive. Those who struggle and fail tend to wheel-spin, don't prioritise and don't apply the magic power of focus.

KEY POINT No. 2: *There's no such thing as lack of time, only lack of focus. We can all do the things we really want to do.*

WHAT CHOICES DO WE HAVE?

It's easy to find problems in our daily life. The boss pushes us into Reactive mode... our partner is always late... our children stress us to the max ... there are always interruptions in our day... the traffic was too heavy today... and we could go on.

At first we tend to think we don't have choices. We feel pushed and pulled by the twists of fate. Not so. We have choice at every step of the way. There are always things we can do – sometimes only small things – that will in the long term make a huge impact in our lives. This includes tiny shifts in understanding, attitude or behaviour.

Somewhere we have to stop and say: *'I'm part of this situation so I am also part of the solution. What can I change?'*

Did you realise that, as soon as you start responding in a slightly different way to any set of circumstances, you alter their effect?
- For instance, you can avoid the morning traffic by leaving earlier and having breakfast in town. You'll side-step rush hour stress and arrive at work relaxed and ready to swing into action.
- Children to organise? Do their lunches the night before and make sure their clothes are laid out. Or, get them up 10 minutes earlier.

Don't buy into the belief that you lack time. That's nonsense. It's all about choice and focus. We can all achieve far more than most of us think possible by focusing on what really matters and pushing back on the myriad of time-stealers that hustle for attention all day long.

Getting a handle on time is not about waving a magic wand – it's a continuous application of small, easy and practical steps.

As I was preparing to run a workshop at a school, one of the senior teachers came into the staffroom.

'I'm so pleased to see you', she laughed. *'I reckon I'm the one that triggered the request for your course. I'm* terrible *at my time management.'* For the next couple of minutes she proceeded to give me examples of how terribly bad her time skills were. At least five times she reaffirmed: *'I'm* terrible *at my time management.'*

I'm usually pretty diplomatic, especially when I've just met someone, but eventually I blurted out, *'Do you* really *want to fix your time problems?'*

'Absolutely!' was the emphatic reply.

'Change your language. Every time you reiterate how terrible you are, your sub-conscious says, "You want terrible time management? Coming right up, honey."'

She walked away looking very thoughtful.

KEY POINT No. 3: *There are always ways to change things, but... if you 'argue for your limitations, sure enough, they're yours'.* **(Richard Bach,** *Illusions***)**

CAUTION – IT'S POSSIBLE TO BE EFFICIENT BUT NOT EFFECTIVE

Many people consider themselves very efficient but have forgotten to take a compass bearing on where they're heading. They're so busy doing things right that they forget to notice whether they are doing the right things.

We can patch up our habits by applying some new time management practises but, if we don't understand *why* we're doing what we're doing, the chance of sustaining those practises is pretty slim once the first flush of enthusiasm passes or when a crisis hits. Those who have not taken this reality check often wonder why long-term peace of mind and personal satisfaction don't follow their improved efficiency. They still feel stressed out, even though they know they're wasting less time on unproductive habits. They regularly feel as though the tail is wagging the dog; that they never seem to catch up, no matter how efficient they've become. Familiar? Such people are almost always focused on how to more efficient but not on how to be most effective. They're not taking the helicopter view.

An effective person achieves the right results with minimum fuss. They're clear about their over-riding purpose and day-to-day objectives. They don't waste time on activities which don't support that purpose.

KEY POINT No. 4: *There's no point in learning to be efficient if we're efficiently doing the wrong things.*

ANYONE YOU KNOW? PITFALLS TO AVOID!

Some people *know* they have a challenge with Time Management.

Others think they're good, but are they? Do you know anyone with any of the following traits?

Uptight Arthur

Arthur is absolutely fanatic about *always* being on time. If others keep him waiting even a minute he starts showing signs of an anxiety attack coming on! Keep him waiting five minutes and his stress levels are soaring! He thinks he's good at time management and so he is on the organisational level, but he's often very uncomfortable to be around, can't relax and be flexible, isn't very good at going with the flow, or re-prioritising when something needs urgent attention or crises come up (which happen in everyone's life). Time controls him, not the other way around.

Frenetic Frances

Here we have the person who is *always* busy – but those around her are never exactly sure what keeps her on her perpetual motion treadmill. Frenetic Frances isn't exactly sure either. She doesn't know how to take time out to recharge, isn't good at putting first things first and seldom stops to reflect on where this endless round of activity is taking her. She certainly achieves quite a bit – but is she achieving what matters? She is always *so busy* being busy!

Lewis the List-Maker

Lewis loves lists. He writes down everything. He never forgets things because it's all been recorded but he's so busy planning and getting organised that effective action often doesn't follow.

Sloppy Samantha

Here we have someone who would traditionally be recognised as bad at time management. She's so relaxed, able to go with the flow and easily distracted that she drives any organised person nuts. She is hardly ever on time, forgets things because writing anything down is *such* a drag and achieves half what she should because she's always good for a chat. Don't rely on Samantha!

In truth, most of us show elements of some of these behaviour styles from time to time. The trick is to recognise what you're doing and fix it!

A WARNING BEFORE WE DIG IN TO SPECIFICS – THE PLACE OF DISCIPLINE!

If you're studying this for a quick fix – you're out of luck and I can't help you! A small amount of self-discipline over a period of time, linked to a determination to change, is the key element in better time management.

Be aware, however, that we can only change one thing at a time. Don't try and improve everything simultaneously – you'll blow yourself away. Choose one area. Work on that for at least 21 days and the change will be well on its way to becoming a habit. Then select another habit.

Don't be too hard on yourself when you slip up – as you will. Praise yourself for what you've achieved and get back to the new habits. How long did you take to learn the old ones? You've practised them for a life-time, haven't you? Don't be unrealistic about how long new habits will take to learn, but don't use that as an excuse either! Winners know they won't reform overnight. They're prepared to take the slow road of small regular improvements in order to build more productive habits.

KEY POINT No. 5: *I will do today what others won't, so I can have tomorrow what others can't!*

CHAPTER 2 THE TOOLBAR OF TIME

It was a few years into the training side of my time management business before I realised that all most people want, in anything but their areas of core responsibility, is ...

> **... just enough information and simple enough processes**
> **to get the immediate problem dealt with,**
> ***not* an overload of 'stuff' they're not ready to hear yet**
> ***or* unnecessarily complex processes.**

This applies even in something as fundamental as the quality of their life and the way they use their time. And many time management programmes and books make it all too complicated.

When I first started learning about better time management practises, back in the late 1980's, I was taught to take ten or fifteen minutes at the beginning of each day to write a list of tasks, then code each one. First we did a broad sort – giving each item an A, B or C dependant on priority, then within each alpha category we allocated numbers. We might have A1, A2 and A 3. In the Bs we might go from B1 to B8. And then the Cs, the lowest priority items, were also coded.

It worked for me and so, when others began to ask me for help, of course I passed the method on. Then I started to notice something. Time after time I'd do follow-up sessions with clients and find that only a tiny percentage of the students had sustained the practise. Eventually the penny dropped! What my students taught *me* was that such a process, no matter how good, is too complex. Only the very linear thinkers like it; everyone else discards it within days. Further on in the book you'll learn a far simpler method that was the origin of this system. It was those list-making folks who made an easy system into something complicated.

KEY POINT No. 6: *Unnecessary complexity is a time waster.*

THE QUALITY OF THE QUESTION DETERMINES THE QUALITY OF THE ANSWER

I'd been teaching and speaking on time management for about six years and the first edition of this book had already been in print for about three years. Then one sunny morning a fabulous question from a 21-year-old, and my 90-second answer, changed the way I explain my topic – forever.

I was crossing beautiful Sydney Harbour in Australia on a ferry with my farming son James and his mate Richard. The boys had just finished university and we were off to Manly Beach for a day of sun, surf, and (for the boys) admiration of beautiful scantily-clad women.

Richard was asking about my work. He leaned forward with interest when I began to explain what I taught.

'Robyn, I constantly struggle with time.' And then his next words were an unexpected gift. *'What's the guts of it?'*

The quality of a question determines the quality of the answer – and that was a superb and very targeted question. I'd never thought of my topic in quite that way but suddenly the answer just popped out. It's been an integral part of my teachings ever since.

Here's the quick response I gave Richard.

There are only four elements and if you haven't got all four areas covered, you'll never get a good handle on your time choices.

   1. The Big Picture

   2. Planning & Prioritising, and that expands to four sub-sections:

       a. Don't get bogged down in the urgent at the expense of the important

       b. Develop a Proactive focus

> c. Plan weekly, at the beginning of the week (or before the week starts)
> d. Every day work your 1-5 daily plan
>
> **3. Tips and Techniques**
>
> **4. Sanity Gaps**
>
> The big picture gives you your goals and where you should spend time. It helps you make the right choices, especially when faced with alternatives. It gives you ***clarity and focus.***
>
> Good planning and prioritising helps you use your time ***effectively.*** If you use your diary as a planning tool, not just a list of appointments, you can regularly include small chunks of bigger goals.
>
> On their own, however, the big picture and planning and prioritising are still not enough. We all know people brilliant at strategy and great at planning and yet they dawdle through life. You also need ***efficiency*** – the fast track techniques, the short cuts, the quick ways to save time.
>
> Some people think that if you're efficient you're time-smart. Not necessarily. Short cuts and good techniques by themselves don't constitute good time management, no matter how smart; it's too easy to efficiently rush around doing the wrong things. But combine shortcuts with the first two and you're getting close.
>
> However, great strategy, great prioritising and great techniques are still not enough. It's just a recipe for a very full diary. You'll run around like a headless chook, in ever-diminishing circles, until you collapse in a very ugly heap of exhaustion. Fill every waking moment and you'll just burn out. We also need sanity gaps. We achieve ***quality of life*** only if we regularly recharge and refresh – when we switch off from our busyness and give both our body and brain a chance to rebuild our depleted energy.

'Wow', said Richard. *'That's easy!'*

I looked at him and said, in some surprise as I realised how simply I'd chunked it out, *'Yes, it is!'*

Think of the four elements as like a computer toolbar with drop-down menus. Use it as a diagnostic. Whether it's you or someone you work with who's challenged with time and productivity, a quick glance at this diagram and you can quickly identify where help is needed.

THE TOOLBAR OF TIME

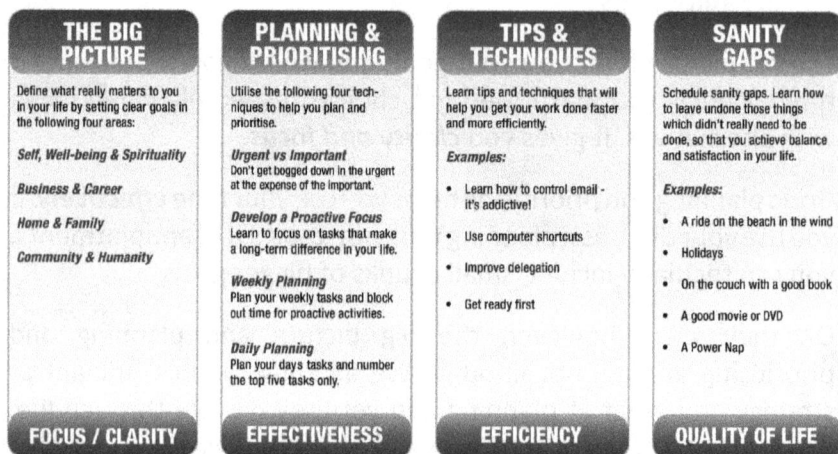

THE BIG PICTURE	PLANNING & PRIORITISING	TIPS & TECHNIQUES	SANITY GAPS
Define what really matters to you in your life by setting clear goals in the following four areas:	Utilise the following four techniques to help you plan and prioritise.	Learn tips and techniques that will help you get your work done faster and more efficiently.	Schedule sanity gaps. Learn how to leave undone those things which didn't really need to be done, so that you achieve balance and satisfaction in your life.
Self, Well-being & Spirituality	*Urgent vs Important* Don't get bogged down in the urgent at the expense of the important.	*Examples:*	*Examples:*
Business & Career	*Develop a Proactive Focus* Learn to focus on tasks that make a long-term difference in your life.	• Learn how to control email - it's addictive!	• A ride on the beach in the wind
Home & Family	*Weekly Planning* Plan your weekly tasks and block out time for proactive activities.	• Use computer shortcuts	• Holidays
Community & Humanity	*Daily Planning* Plan your days tasks and number the top five tasks only.	• Improve delegation	• On the couch with a good book
		• Get ready first	• A good movie or DVD
			• A Power Nap
FOCUS / CLARITY	**EFFECTIVENESS**	**EFFICIENCY**	**QUALITY OF LIFE**

Created by Robyn Pearce (The Time Queen)
Grab your FREE Report 'How To Master Time In Only 90 Seconds' (valued at $35) at *www.gettingagrip.com*

Now, since you're not a testosterone-filled young man on a ferry, heading off to sun and gorgeous scantily-clad bodies, let's take a few chapters to expand the first two of these elements – the Big Picture and Planning and Prioritising. We'll pick up on Tips and Techniques and Sanity Gaps in Part Two.

CHAPTER 3 THE BIG PICTURE

We all know about goals. Most accept that there is merit in goalsetting. Many have experienced success in this area – and yet a surprising number of people (including those who've already achieved goals in the past) don't have a *current* list of clear goals. And amongst those who do have goals, even less have written them down.

I was like that once – and I now *love* the incredible difference clear goals make. Without them we're like a rudderless boat, pushed and pulled by the winds of fate. Yes, we'll still quite likely have a nice life but how sad would it be, when we're about to pop our mortal coil, to be filled with regrets for what might have been. Do you want to be one of those unfilled old people saying, *'If only I'd done ...'* or *'I wish I'd given ... a go?'*

THE KICK IN THE GUTS THAT INTRODUCED ME TO GOALSETTING

In my days of single parenthood, living near a small country town and surviving on government handouts, I knew nothing about success principles. I was that rudderless boat, getting by from day to day. But once I learnt about goalsetting, life changed dramatically.

I'm a qualified librarian by my first career choice, but by the time this story opens I'd spent fifteen of the previous eighteen years being a farmer's wife and raising six kids. Five I birthed and an intellectually handicapped foster son completed the package. I'd only returned to the workforce three years prior, forced by economic necessity after my marriage broke up. However, in that small provincial town the only job I could get that even partly used my qualifications was a part-time teacher aide position in a school library – at very low pay on a government work scheme.

I was grateful for the job and the school hours were great as far as the children were concerned. However, I was weary of the endless efforts to keep things together on a subsistence income. We were just above the breadline – an ice-cream for everyone once a week was the height of luxury! One day I noticed an ad in the local paper for a new town librarian. I became very excited. At last – a chance to get off the poverty trap. The previous incumbent, another solo mother (and this point is relevant to the story!) had just run off under rather dramatic circumstances with a local headmaster.

I rushed in an application. Here was a chance for me to practise my vocation properly – I *knew* I was a good librarian.

My strongest competition was the woman already caretaking the position. She was also the wife of a well-liked and respected local businessman. However, I soon found out that I was the only qualified candidate – the other lady was just *thinking* about doing the library exams whereas I'd spent five years training and working in larger libraries further south before becoming a child-raising machine. Surely, if there was any justice in the world, I would get the job!

The interview with twelve local dignitaries – businesspeople and council representatives – came and went. It was pretty intimidating but, full of hope, I went home and waited – and waited – and waited.

Days went by. Why were they taking so long? Where was the letter, where was the phone call?

Nearly a week later, still hoping, I drove into town for groceries. A neighbour was meandering down the other side of the road. She spotted me. *'Robyn'*, she called out, waving vigorously. Clearly she wanted me to cross over for a chat. Surprised, for we weren't close friends, I obeyed the summons.

With no preamble, she said importantly, *'Have you heard about the library job?'*

'No', I replied, somewhat puzzled. I knew that in a small town the grapevine was often faster than the mail, but this was a strange messenger. She had nothing to do with the council and certainly hadn't been on the selection panel.

'*Oh*', she said, puffing with pleasure at being the first, '*they decided not to give you the job – they reckon solo mothers are unreliable.*'

I held back my tears until out of sight of her malicious eyes. But – what a favour those risk-averse people did me.

Two things happened.

The first was a fiery determination – '*I'll show the bastards!*' (I didn't know how but I wasn't going to take that slap lying down!)

The second was one of those serendipitous events that just 'happen' and my first real introduction to goalsetting. A friend loaned me *Creative visualisation: use the power of your imagination to create what you want in your life* by Shakti Gawain – and it changed my life. In a few short pages it opened up a whole new world. I discovered success principles taught by wisdom writers in every culture and faith over countless centuries. For the first time I realised that I didn't need to just go with the flow; I didn't need to be that ship without a rudder; I didn't have to just 'take what comes'. There were principles I could apply that would help me create the kind of life I really wanted.

Within a year I was out of the town and in a better-paid job. Within two years I was in a major city and in the real estate career I mentioned earlier – sometimes earning more in a month than I'd earned in a year on government handouts.

IN WHAT DIRECTION DO YOU WANT TO GO?

If we don't know the answer to this question, if we don't have clear goals or a vision for where we want our life to go, how can we possibly be sure we've made the right decisions on a daily basis when faced with multiple time choices? That clarity gives us the confidence to prioritise effectively. In a business context it gives us the ability to stay strategic with our focus – keeping on task with the important few activities that will make the long-term difference.

Every day we have to make decisions. '*Shall I do this or shall I do that?*' There's no shortage of good ideas and fascinating by-ways to distract us. (I'm still tempted from time to time!) However, a clear picture of our possible future life gives us far greater power to say '*no*' or to push back in an appropriate way. (Not in a career-limiting or relationship-limiting way, I hasten to add!)

EXAMPLES OF 'NO'
- '*Sorry but my time commitments don't allow me to do that.*'
- '*Sounds great but that's not the focus of my business right now.*'
- '*I love the idea but I wouldn't be able to give that project the focus you deserve.*'
- To a manager attempting to overload you: '*I'm on ..... (projects) right now. I'm happy to take this new one on, but which of the others would you like me to defer?*'
- '*I'll be free to start this in ....* (Give a realistic time frame). *Is that ok or do you need to ask someone else to take it on?*'
- To a family member or friend: '*I'd love to but I've already made a commitment to do something else.*' (You don't necessarily have to explain what that other commitment is. It might be to have some 'me' time! We'll talk more about this in Chapter 13 Sanity Gaps.)

KEY POINT No. 7: *'No' is your most powerful time management tool.*

WHY MANY PEOPLE DON'T HAVE CLEAR GOALS
There are a number of concerns – people worry about possible failure, what others might say if they aim for something really big, or it hasn't worked in the past. But the biggest story by far is that people say they don't have time.

What they're really saying is that something as important as the rest of our lives deserves serious consideration and they assume it will take a lot of time (which they don't have spare right now) to do the thinking. Well, that's half-true. It is very important but – it doesn't need to take long.

The block for most people is in not knowing exactly *what* they want. There seem to be too many choices.

One major reason why so many people don't have clarity is that they don't realise there's more than one way to set goals.

Many people feel hemmed in by traditional goalsetting. It feels too rigid and structured. They find it frustrating and crushing to the spirit. Some try it for a while and then return quietly to the old habit of going with the flow. Others never try at all because it all seems too hard!

Here's the thing, dear reader. Would you take half an hour to have a coffee with a friend? If I could show you how, in the same amount of time, you could have a delicious and exciting list of goals totally personal to yourself, why wouldn't you do it? This is the rest of your life we're talking about, buddy!

(And, once you've done it you'll have all the information you need to get maximum value from this book.)

What I encourage you to focus on here is not the SMART goalsetting commonly written about and which we'll talk about later.

The Big Picture goalsetting is more flexible and wide-ranging. To start with, we just need a simple way to tap our sub-conscious into the long-term future. There's no right or wrong. It doesn't matter if we don't achieve everything off the list, or in the time-frames we initially plan for. And it's more fun! It's also a way of setting objectives that works extremely well for many different personality styles. It allows us to be open to opportunities, rather than focused on rigid deadlines. It takes goalsetting out of the 'have-to-do' category. This is not to say we won't choose to be disciplined about sticking to our action plans, but it does recognise that rigid adherence to a plan sometimes locks us into struggle and activity that may no longer be relevant.

This more relaxed style of goalsetting also takes away the sense of pressure, anxiety and often guilt (a wasteful and unnecessary emotion) which some people experience when they're struggling to achieve, or don't achieve, everything they've aimed for. Even very logical folk find it very energising and empowering.

Stuart Wilde, in his little book *Life was never meant to be a struggle* says: *'The struggler sees only the goal, not the path. He is trapped by his opinion of how to reach the goal. No other possibilities exist. So life moves out of his way, leaving him to operate in a barren land. The struggler is forced to head in the direction he has set for himself. Often, in his frantic effort to make his goal, he misses the side turning that would offer simplicity or a short cut. [He]... ploughs on regardless of pain and anguish or whether his actions are appropriate or effective.'*

SIMPLE STEPS TO QUICKLY DISCOVER YOUR BIG PICTURE GOALS

(If you already have a current list, you might like to review them as we whistle through the next few chapters.)

1. **Find a quiet spot.**
   Don't attempt it with other people making noise around you – you must have dedicated thinking time. Introspection might not be easy the first time but the power that comes out of the exercise far exceeds the discomfort of learning to look inward.

2. **Think at least a year out (and further ahead if you can).**
   Write down in very specific language, with as much detail as possible, goals in the following four life areas*. I think you'll find these four categories cover most of life, but if there is any other major life area not covered, add it to your own list:
   • Self, Wellbeing and Spirituality
   • Business and Career
   • Home and Family
   • Community and Humanity
   *Footnote: If you'd like further help, check out our Getting a Grip on Life – Goals Toolkit. (See Resources.) It's a filtering tool with a series of questions and exercises to help you really nail exactly what you want.)

3. **If something comes into your mind, don't dismiss it with thoughts of: *'I can't do that'*, or *'It's not practical'*.**
   Listen to your intuition. Perhaps you've been in the habit of squashing your dreams. If you feel a lightness and inner excitement you can bet your boots that your subconscious is trying to tell you something. Such feelings are signposts.

4. **Initially do goals for yourself, not the others in your life.**
   It's not selfish – it's just easier. If other people will be involved with some of them, negotiate later. Some timelines may have to be

shifted but you need to be clear on your own thoughts before you can have a useful conversation with someone else.

5. **Nothing is too small or too large.**
A small thing can sometimes be the trigger that leads to the fulfilment of a much bigger goal. For example, a successful weight-loss result for an over-weight person almost always results in a major lift in self-esteem. Time after time you hear of those same people subsequently achieving amazing things that they'd really thought were beyond them.

6. **Don't limit yourself – forget 'realistic'.**
The more linear form of goalsetting uses that SMART acronym I mentioned earlier – Specific, Measurable, Achievable, Realistic and Time-Bound (or similar words). It's a useful guide for things you want to achieve soon. They might include sales targets, monthly budgets, a short-term savings goal, sports achievements, losing weight or something you wish to do round the house. We also apply it with weekly planning, as we'll discuss soon. However, it's entirely too limiting for long-term dream goals. Who wants to be realistic? Or only choose goals that are easily achievable? Where's the challenge and excitement in that!

Instead, dream big. It isn't your imminent projects or relatively easy activities we're interested in at this stage. They come later. This is the time to throw logic to the winds and listen to your heart.

Have you ever heard of John Goddard? Read his Life List in *The Original Chicken Soup for the Soul* or at www.johngoddard.info/ life_list.htm. He was 15 when he commenced that list. At age 74 he'd done 109 of the 127 items on his list.

He became a world-famous wildlife writer, photographer and scientific explorer. He travelled to 120 countries, flew 47 different types of aircraft, set several civilian air-speed records, piloted a submarine, climbed many of the major mountains of the world, swam in a number of the largest lakes, navigated the length of the Nile, the Congo, the Amazon, rode a camel, climbed the pyramids, read the Bible from cover to cover, the complete works of Shakespeare, most of the Encyclopaedia Britannica – and many more achievements. When asked by a reporter how he'd had such an amazing life he answered, '*It was starting my list.*'

And you'll have your own list of people who've set their sights high, dreamed the 'impossible dream' and subsequently gone on to achieve amazing results. Rather than turn this into a biographical list of amazing people who've achieved the seemingly impossible, I leave you with just two – Nelson Mandela and Barack Obama. Nothing more I need to say, is there!

7. **Write them down.**
Many people will say, '*Oh, I know what's important to me. Why do I need to record it?*'

Have you noticed that the exercise of putting your thoughts down on paper forces clarity? A landscaper on one of my courses had this to say about writing down his goals: '*I remember when I started. It was very difficult at first to make myself begin to write. It took me a long time to work out why but I finally identified two reasons.*

'*For one thing, it takes self-discipline to sit and do the writing. We live in a busy world, a world of instant action and quick entertainment. It's easier to cruise through life with a comfortable but only general awareness of what our most important issues are.*

'*And secondly, somehow writing them down made them more serious. It was like making a commitment, even if only to myself. Finally I realised that it felt scary. I'd been afraid of what I might find when I looked more closely inside my head. In fact, it was a very liberating experience, once I started.*'

8. **Be very specific.**
Don't say '*I want more money*', '*I want a new house*', or '*I want to travel*'. Instead specify how much. Describe what the house will look like. What atmosphere? How many rooms? Do you want a garden? Where will you travel? For how long? What specific activities do you wish to do when you're there?

In 1996 my second husband Mike was transferred to a new job in Sydney, Australia. I took another six months to close down my business in New Zealand and be free to join him. His choice of accommodation was an inner-suburb high-rise apartment – rugby football ground across the road (the dream of many red-blooded Kiwi guys!), a good range of restaurants and a movie theatre only two minutes' walk away, no garden, no maintenance – convenience was paramount. He was out at work all day – who cared about atmosphere as long as it was convenient?

I finally made the transition, leaving tenants in our comfortable two-storey family home with wonderful garden in a leafy quiet suburb and a lovely wide-ranging view of city, bush and a distant view of the sea.

I arrived to a sterile high-rise apartment block. The outlook consisted of a car park below and seven other apartment blocks. To exercise anywhere interesting I had to catch a bus or train. The only neighbour I saw regularly was an odd-looking fellow in the apartment block directly across the car park who spent half the day smoking on his balcony and staring over at me (when he got the chance). I knew virtually no-one in the whole of Australia, had no work, very little money, no car and a busy husband working long hours.

I hated it! For the first week poor Mike came home day after day to a homesick wife in tears (and I don't do either tears or homesick!) Something had to change, and fast.

I knew enough about goalsetting by then to make a list of the qualities and features of the new apartment I wanted. It included words such as: quiet, peaceful, atmosphere, small building, nice neighbours, close to transport, within fifteen minutes of the inner city outside peak traffic, near water and affordable. (I didn't know the cost of rentals in Sydney then so was blissfully unaware that 'affordable' didn't fit with some of the other descriptors on my list!)

The very next Saturday we went looking. Within two hours we found a delightful little apartment in a small eight-unit, two-storey complex tucked away in a quiet leafy street. It was only five minutes' walk from Balmoral Beach, one of the prettiest beaches in Sydney – *and* within our tight budget range. Had I accepted conventional wisdom and just focused on 'affordable' we wouldn't have even *looked* in that area.

Be specific in every detail and then expect miracles!

9. **Find or make pictures to represent your words and thoughts.**
Make a collage, a poster, a scrapbook or some kind of visual reminder. Pictures are incredibly powerful. Put them wherever you'll see them constantly – it might be your fridge, your office wall or maybe your bathroom. After a while they'll become wallpaper and you'll hardly notice them most of the time. However, the message continues to impact your sub-conscious. It might take some years, but one day you'll look back in amazement.

Many years ago, my friend Maggie invited me to a Life Map party. I wondered what on earth I was letting myself in for.

She led us through a process of identifying and writing down our dream goals. (She'd just read *The Original Chicken Soup for the Soul* and been inspired by not only John Goddard's story but also Glenna Salsbury's *Goal Book* – both stories are in that original *Chicken Soup*). She gave each of us a big sheet of coloured card, a pile of magazines, scissors and glue.

It was fun. A couple of hours later I went home with a lovely sheet of yummy things I wanted to have 'one day'. As well as a lot of travel and other things it included a picture of a small white house only a few steps from a quiet little sandy beach and a pretty inner harbour. Trees were dotted around the house, two small boats were moored a few metres off the beach and the feeling flowing from the scene was one of serenity and peace.

At the time Mike and I were early in our relationship. There were always multiple candidates for every penny to be spent – a beach house was *not* anywhere on the horizon and nor could I see it happening at any time in the foreseeable future. But – *'dreams are free'* I thought to myself; I certainly knew I *wanted* to live by water. I could *feel* myself in that lovely setting.

Years went by. We moved to Australia, as I've just told you. And then, after four happy years we returned to Auckland to be nearer to the increasing family – the first two of the subsequent seventeen grandchildren had arrived and I didn't want to be an absentee grandmother.

Fifteen years after that Life Map party, Mike and I decided one summer's day to take a drive out into the surrounding country. He was sceptical but I wanted to see if we could find anything close to water that maybe, just maybe, we could afford. As we approached the first harbourside community on my list, a small hand-written sign on a fence caught our eye. It said '*Section for Sale. 525 square metres.*' (That's pretty small!) It was down a short side road we didn't even know existed.

Two minutes later we found it. The tide was in, the sun was shining and the two pohutukawa (sometimes fondly described as the New Zealand Christmas tree) fronting the property were proudly displaying their gorgeous crimson flowers against the rich green foliage. The little piece of land was sitting empty and pristine – just waiting for someone to fall in love. That someone was me!

I live there now. The purchase wasn't smooth but as complications arose I kept on seeing myself sitting on the future deck, wine glass in hand, watching the sunset go down over the bay. I even went so far as to write down my name and future address – over and over.

Three years later, house designed, built and living in it, I was cleaning out some old boxes. I found the Life Map I'd made all those years ago at Maggie's house. There was that little white beach house I'd cut out all those years ago. Shivers went down my spine. It wasn't the same location. It wasn't the same house. But the essence of both the house and the property was *exactly* the same – serene, peaceful and tree-fringed. And, two boats are almost always moored across the bay.

Goal setting is an important step in what's to come, so please be sure to do it now.

KEY POINT No. 8: *A clear set of goals, knowing what's important TO ME, helps me make wise time choices.*

As we study how the brain and mind work, we realize that the process of holding a dream or a vision clearly in mind is the first step toward finding the path from current reality to this new reality.

We now know that neuro-chemically, when we hold an exciting or inspiring dream
clearly in mind, the chemical makeup in our brain changes, which actually transforms the way we think.

Ann McGee-Cooper & Duane Trammell *Time Management for Unmanageable People*

COMMITMENT

Until one is committed, there is the chance to draw back, always ineffectiveness. Concerning all acts of initiative (and creation) there is one elementary truth, the ignorance of which kills countless ideas and splendid plans – that the moment one definitely commits oneself, then providence moves too.

All sorts of things occur to help one that would not otherwise have occurred.
A whole stream of events issue from the decision, raising in one's favour all manner of unforeseen incidents and meetings and material assistance which no man could have dreamed would come his way.

I have learnt a deep respect for one of Goethe's couplets:
'Whatever you can do or dream you can, begin it.
Boldness has genius, magic and power in it'.

W.H. Murray. *The Scottish Himalaya Expedition.* (1951)

Twenty years from now you will be more disappointed by the things you didn't do than by the ones you did do.

So throw off the bowlines. Sail away from the safe harbour.
Catch the trade winds in your sails.
Explore. Dream. Discover.

Mark Twain

And one last quote from Napoleon Hill, author of *Think and Grow Rich.* This book is one of the world's bestsellers of all time and studied vigorously by almost every successful entrepreneur.

All the great leaders, in all walks of life and during all periods of history, have attained their leadership by the application of their abilities behind a definite major purpose.

It is no less impressive to observe that those who are classified as failures have no such purpose, but go around and around, like a ship without a rudder, coming back always empty-handed to their starting point.

CHAPTER 4 PLANNING AND PRIORITISING

URGENCY – THE FALSE FRIEND

During the Second World War General Eisenhower is reported as saying that very few urgent things were ever really important, and conversely, very few important things were ever urgent. And yet how often do we allow the urgent 'stuff' to crack the whip! Take a mental check right now. How much of your life is consumed with urgencies?

Here's the secret – even if we've got heaps of urgent stuff going down, somehow we have to push back on some of it in order to work on more of the longer-term important but less urgent activities. If we do, we start to take more control. That's where the change comes from. If we don't, we're stuck in Frenetic busy work for ever. Not a pretty thought, is it!

Of course some things are urgent. They'll include crises, deadlines, accidents and fixing up important matters that have gone wrong. They're the 'few' that General Eisenhower talked about and of course must be attended to immediately.

Now analyse the rest of your screaming deadlines. Everything seems urgent, doesn't it? And email makes it worse. In your heart of hearts you know the situation won't change and the deadlines won't go away – if you carry on with the same routines. But *how* to make that shift – there's the big question.

As you learn to take control of this habit of being urgency-focused you'll achieve major benefits. However, if you remain stuck in the crazy tyranny of the urgent there's no head space to make those changes.

Merrill and Donna Douglass in *Manage your time, your work, yourself* (first published in 1980 and revised and republished several times) had this to say:

We live in constant tension between the urgent and the important. Our problem is that important things seldom must be done today, or even this week. Important things are seldom urgent. Urgent things, however, call for our attention – making endless demands of us, applying pressure every hour, every day.

We seldom question urgent things, never knowing for sure whether they are really urgent or only masquerading as urgent. And sometimes we develop the habit of responding as if they were urgent when they're not. Many apparently urgent things are indeed masqueraders. What we need is the wisdom, the courage and discipline to do the important things first. If we can break the tyranny of the urgent, we can solve our time dilemma.

AN INSIDIOUS ADDICTION

Did you know that many people are addicted to urgency? How familiar is this scene?

Tom has a big project to complete. It's due in two weeks. He knows it will take about ten hours. So he starts it two days before D-Day, has to take work home because of the number of inconsiderate (!) interruptions he experiences at the office and at the last minute, under considerable pressure and stress, completes the task.

In his heart of hearts he knows he could have done a better job if he'd started earlier. However, it was if a huge brick wall blocked him from starting.

He always has such good intentions but they never seem to win. His explanation is, '*I always work better under pressure*' and '*Deadlines suit me*'.

You've heard it all before, haven't you!

The truth is, Tom is addicted to stress and last-minute pressure. If you gave him twice as long to prepare, it would still be done at the last minute. He doesn't know how to function without pressure and is so uncomfortable without it that he wastes time on inconsequential time-filling activities. When the pressure comes on again the adrenalin starts to flow, his energy levels rise, and – like an alcoholic with a bottle almost within reach – he starts to move.

How do I know this scene so well? I've been there.

In my early years I was the female version of Tom. However, as I developed more awareness of the benefits of operating from a Proactive position, the dependence on stress and pressure to get me moving began to fade. The pleasure of being on time for things and being ready in advance for events and deadlines became stronger and stronger, the more I achieved. Taking one small step at a time, I practised saying 'no' to old habits of last-minuting and putting myself under pressure. Now, the old comfortable habits are uncomfortable. I don't feel good when I slip up. Every now and then, a little nasty from the past sneaks under my guard, just to keep me humble. It reminds me of what it felt like to be nearly always late for everything!

I'm glad to say no one, no matter how addicted to stress and urgency they are, has to stay in that addiction mode. The answer is in your own hands – but more than anything, you have to *want* to change and be prepared to do something about it.

Those lucky readers who've always been organised souls won't understand what we're talking about, but believe me, it is a very real problem for many people.

In the following pages we'll look at how we can shift from this state of urgency to gain back more control over our time, our life and our results.

THE ANTIDOTE TO URGENCY – DEVELOP A PROACTIVE FOCUS

People who take control of their circumstances, who attend to the important activities instead of allowing urgent matters to control them, are Proactive. They don't feel out of control, pushed and pulled by everyone else's demands.

For instance:

- If they don't enjoy their work they will go out and find a new job.
- Instead of automatically accepting that the current way of doing things is the best and only way, they actively look for improved methods.
- They're good at pushing back on tasks or activities that don't fit with their long-term plans and goals.
- They don't jump every time the phone rings, chirps or beeps. Instead they attend to such items at a time that suits them.

Most Proactive activities, again linking back to General Eisenhower's definition, are of low urgency and long-term importance. The problem is, unless we deliberately focus on them, they sit quietly in the wings and are easy to overlook. They don't usually shout and yell at us. They're opportunities that will quietly slip away unnoticed as we race frenetically around doing our 'busy' work.

A Reactive person, on the other hand, passively accepts what comes, even when they don't like it. They tend to feel controlled by the urgencies of everyday life and seem unable to reach beyond the immediate. It's uncomfortable to attend first to the actions that will make the biggest difference, instead of the noisy 'urgencies'.

As we develop a Proactive focus, our tendency to be addicted to urgency reduces. So how can we break that tyranny trap, for many people struggle with it?

Have a look at the following diagram. It's a very powerful tool and has been used in various forms by many time management writers over many years. In 1980 Merrill and Donna Douglas and then, more recently, writers such as Brian Tracy and Stephen Covey made it well-known. I've added my own modifications for ease of understanding. It highlights our various types of daily activity, their relative importance and where we need to focus in order to break that urgency trap.

Vital Urgent	High ←	Urgency	→ Low	Vital Not urgent

	Frenetic/Pressing	**Proactive/Value-Adding**
High ↑ Importance ↓ Low	High Urgency High Importance	Low Urgency High Importance
	High Urgency Low Importance	Low Urgency Low Importance
	Reactive/Responsive	**Time-wasting**

Urgent
Not vital

Not urgent
Not vital

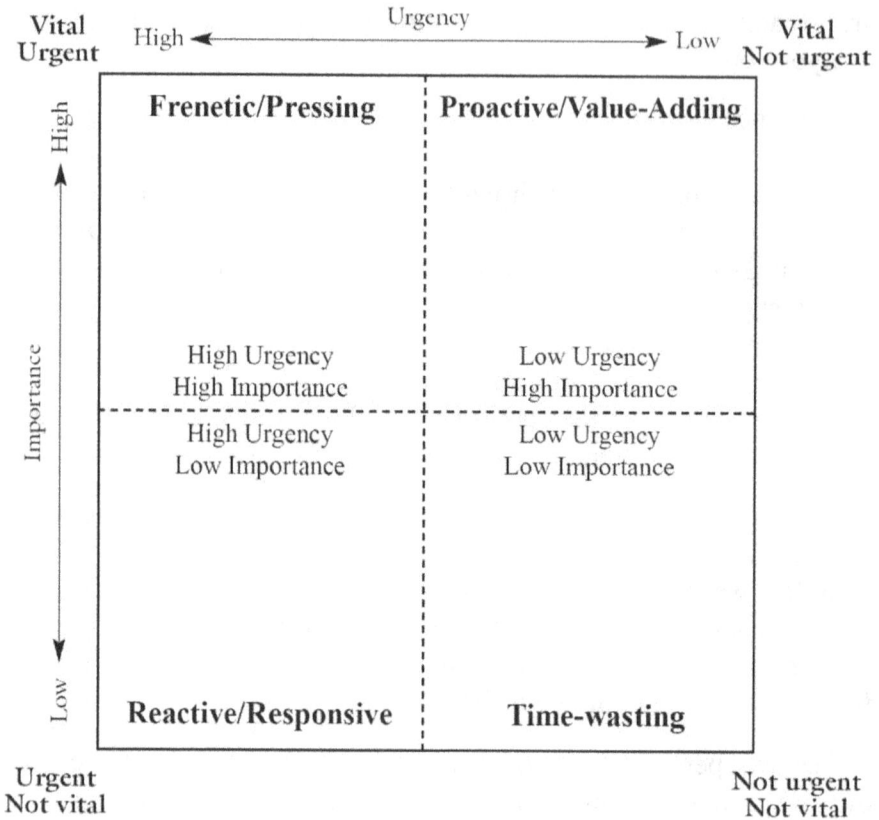

Action Styles Diagram.

Frenetic or Pressing activities – highly urgent and highly important

Activities that fit into this sector include:

- Any sort of deadline
- Crises
- Fire-fighting, because something wasn't done properly the first time
- Usually things which haven't been planned for, or should have been planned for and weren't

It's certainly not all negative, which is why I include the word 'pressing'. Sometimes we *choose* to work out of this high focus sector. Think of when you're heading off on holiday. It can be very energising to get things done at a very fast pace, knowing we can then relax.

It does not include items which have been planned and prepared for, such as appointments, meetings, or anything else which was scheduled **and for which you are ready**.

> My definition of this sector:
> ***Anything which must be done today and no***
> ***responsible person***
> ***would leave it undone.***

Reactive or Responsive activities – highly urgency (to someone else) but of (relatively) low importance to you

Here we have:
- Interruptions and unexpected visitors
- A large percentage of paperwork
- Some meetings (or parts of)
- Some phone calls (or parts of)
- Much email
- 'Stuff'. (Don't you love that word? So encompassing!)

Most of us have a multitude of these items. They never go away and we never seem to catch up. In general terms they are other people's urgencies, not our own. Or they may be interesting but will have a relatively low impact on your top priorities and responsibilities. Many people spend the bulk of their day in this category. It's very easy to fall into the trap of hours vanishing while we beaver away being Reactive.

KEY POINT No. 9: *Beware of majoring in minor things.*

If your work involves supporting others, rather than initiating things

Your job might be to attend to other people's needs, doing some combination of the tasks listed above. Customer service, handling complaints, warranty work, retail, PA and receptionist work are examples. The trigger for the tasks may still be other people's urgencies, but they can be handled in a *Responsive* rather than *Reactive* way. For instance, by seeking for improved ways to provide your service, you're operating from a Proactive perspective rather than a *'I do what I'm told'* mindset. And the spin-off is that, by taking an active interest in your work there's a very good chance of either promotion or further opportunities elsewhere, due to your increased competence and skills.

The responsive travel agent

About nine months after I moved to Australia, beginning my time management business afresh in my new country, I was asked to speak at the annual convention of a nation-wide travel agency.

Although the event was still two months away, I began my preparation. After some research and a site visit to a nearby office I asked the people at Head Office for the name of a 'best practise' agent. I was looking for industry-specific and company-specific time-saving methods. When, as a speaker, you only have one hour with an audience, using some of their own terminology and examples is always the fastest way to get the message across.

I was given the name of a young woman who was one of the most effective and top-selling agents in the firm. She worked on the other side of Sydney, a long way from me. The following morning, just before 9am, I gave her a call. She was unavailable so I left a comprehensive message, explaining what I wanted and mentioning that Head Office had given me permission to call. That evening, about 6pm, she returned my call. This time it was I who got a message – I'd left my office a little earlier.

The next morning around the same time, I called again. Same result – I only got as far as the receptionist. This time I just left a short message. She replied again at the end of the day – 5.30pm this time. Fortunately I was still at my desk. We had a very useful half-hour conversation, during which she gave me a bundle of really excellent and valuable information.

From that experience I gained a really valuable distinction about the difference between Reactive and Responsive.

There's a number of ways that young woman could have handled my call. She could have been Reactive by:
- Calling back quickly when she saw the words 'Head Office'. Many people knee-jerk when anything official shows up.

- Or she could have thought: *'That's a bother – I'll deal with it right away and get that woman off my back'*. If so, I'm sure her information would have been minimal. Travel agencies are always busy and she would not have been free to talk for very long.
- Or she could have even ignored the call. After all, it was unlikely that she'd get any business from it. It was before the days of internet bookings and most people worked with agents nearby. She would have noticed by the phone number that I was right across town – about two hours' drive away.

Instead, she was very Responsive:

- She didn't knee-jerk her response.
- She called back at a time convenient to her.
- She had time to think about what she wanted to say. (I'd made that easy by giving enough detail in my comprehensive first message.)
- And most important of all – she called outside of commercial hours. She hadn't become one of the top sellers of the company by accident. One of her disciplines was not doing non-commercial activities in commercial time, unless there was nothing else to do. Especially in those pre-internet days, travel agency work was done in office hours with people either face-to-face or over the phone. She stayed focused on her work during work time and dealt with the other 'stuff' when no more customers would call.

> After that experience, I expanded my definition of this sector into two questions:
>
> **First, *'Is this my responsibility?'***
> **If the answer is yes, then,**
> ***'When is the best time to do it?'***

Next time someone comes at you with one of their (seemingly) urgent tasks, ask yourself those two questions before you jump in. You might be surprised how much time it saves you.

Time-Wasting activities – low urgency and low importance
These activities include:

- Any sort of trivial time-wasters.

- An *excessive* amount of anything, such as television, light reading, time at the pub, computer games, or anything else **taken to excess**.
- Perfectionism – which leads to apparent procrastination. If we're too fixated on making something perfect it will appear that we're procrastinating.
- Too many coffee breaks, long lunches and other enjoyable but irrelevant little by-ways such as organising office sweepstakes or football pools (unless you're the Social Club secretary).

They may be perfectly acceptable activities in themselves, but when we spend too much time on them we're right down in Time-wasting mode. In our heart of hearts we always know when we're wandering down this fascinating by-way. In general, time-wasters are things which, if we didn't do them, would make no difference to our life – in fact, doing them may have a negative impact because we've allowed them to replace other more productive activities.

Consider:
- What is the 'lost opportunity' cost?
- What else could you be doing with that chunk of time?

> My definition of this sector:
> ***Anything taken to excess.***

Proactive activities – low urgency and high importance

This is the category of work that many people dodge around and tend to leave until last. It is, however, the key to effective time management. Master this sector and you master yourself.

The activities include:
1. Weekly and daily planning.
2. Forward long-term planning.
3. Developing strategies to prevent or reduce crises.
4. Further education and study.
5. Development of new products and programmes.
6. Company time spent brainstorming solutions to common problems.

7. Implementation of those solutions.
8. Process and system improvements.
9. Delegation. (More about this in Chapter 9).
10. Cultivation of new clients (and almost every industry needs them).
11. Relationships – both personal and business ones.
12. Re-creation, including time alone as well as with loved ones.
13. Health.
14. Sport and exercise.
15. Financial planning.
16. Hobbies.

The more we focus on being Proactive with our day, our week and our life the more in control we feel.

- How many people do you know whose focus is on Proactive activities? They'll be easy to identify.
- Do *you* focus on Proactive activities?

KEY POINT No. 10: Constantly ask yourself: '*What is my highest priority right now?*'

Most people spend their lives oscillating between Frenetic and Reactive, with an occasional dip into Time-Wasting for light relief. (I spent many years doing the same!) Working regularly and consistently on Proactive tasks initially seems like hard work – until you start to get some rewards. It's a bit like pushing through the pain barrier when you begin to get fit after a long period of inactivity.

My definition of this sector:
Anything that will make a positive long-term difference in your life.

KEY POINT No. 11: *Focus on the vital few things that make a long-term difference.*

SOME PRACTICAL EXAMPLES OF PROACTIVE ACTIVITIES:

- Doing a new edition of this book is a classic example. It would be much easier to just not bother. The original version is still an excellent read. However, as the years have gone by and I've learnt and experienced new things, the first book has become further and further divorced from what I now teach.

  I can assure you, it's infinitely easier to deal with day-to-day tasks than give my first 'child' a makeover. It's a bit like renovating a house – often harder to do over than to start from scratch! Quite a bit of the time my rebellious self wanted to behave like one of my grandkids – resist the work and go play. But my disciplined self won!

- In one of my seminars a parent shared how his son's teacher made a practise of praising every child in her room every day. By doing so, she built up the self-esteem of her pupils, and encouraged the behaviour she wanted them to exhibit. Result – previously difficult students were putty in her hands and she didn't have to waste precious time on negative discipline.

  When I shared that with a group of teachers, one quite senior man looked at me askance and blurted out, *'You wouldn't have time to do that'*. I suspect that quite a bit of his time was spent on discipline and control.

- A freight forwarding company realised, while doing a *Getting a Grip on the Paper War* course with me, that if they shifted a photocopier and large table into another area they would have better paper flow and a more pleasant and productive working environment.

  They also realised that their archival storage had turned into a tip for anything that people didn't want around their workspace but were reluctant to take responsibility for throwing out. They delegated someone with a good systematic mind to sort, file and label. The rubbish disappeared and with the new labels everyone could easily see where to place new archival items and where to *replace* items they'd used and wanted to return. Their information retrieval processes immediately worked faster and

more efficiently, instead of adding to the stress of already very busy people.
- An international firm always had huge pressure at month end, when accounts had to be closed off, data processed and final figures relayed to the parent body in America. During a group discussion the Accounts Department realised that by slightly re-arranging staff schedules and equipment they could do the job within working hours. Previously, six people had given up evenings and weekends at the end of every month to close off the figures.

The team also identified that if each of them gave the CFO (Chief Financial Officer) a breakdown of their work timetables and due dates for vital work she could create a better work-flow pattern for everyone.

The few hours dedicated to finding and solving these issues had a major impact on the efficiency of the company, improved staff morale and saved many hours and a lot of money.
- Kate's division of an international consumer goods company was in the midst of a major reshuffle, involving people in both Australia and New Zealand. The New Zealand General Manager (we'll call her Jane) was tasked with heading up the integration.

A helicopter view of the habits of the extra people she'd just become responsible for showed some clear opportunities for productivity improvement. The merge of two departments was about to create a huge amount of extra work for a short time and Jane didn't want people burning out, nor did she want a poor result. She'd used my coaching and consultancy services for some years so brought me in for a six-month contract to help the combined team of fourteen people iron out inefficiencies and make a smooth transition.

Kate was bogged down with too much time in meetings. By applying three simple techniques (and I'll share them and other examples with you in the chapter on meetings) the next week she saved herself eight hours – an entire work day! Outcome: the most productive week she'd had in ages and a saving of thousands of dollars to the firm because of the other work she was freed up to do, not only that week but on into the future. And that was only one of many dollar and time-savings the team made.

The impact on the company was huge, both financially and in morale. They had to slow down to do the training and coaching but the gains far outweighed the time and money invested.

Almost every company has work-flow efficiencies waiting to be discovered but typically they're too busy doing 'business as usual'. An outsider, on the other hand, can see the gaps very easily. When someone says, '*You can't do that here*' an external consultant will ask, '*Why?*' and '*Why not?*' If you can't afford to hire in a coach or external consultant, learn to think like one. Ask yourself the 'Why' and 'Why Not?' questions, and don't be fobbed off with the first answers (even when they're yours!).

As you develop a Proactive mindset you'll find you become a walking question mark, always looking for the improvements that will make a difference, even if only a few minutes per day.

KEY POINT No. 12: *In order to go faster, first you must go slower.*

THAT SMART ITALIAN, SENOR PARETO

There's one more thing to consider before we dig into the specifics of how to plan our week and then our day.

Have you heard of the Pareto Principle? Or the 80/20 rule? Same thing.

In 1906 Vilfredo Pareto, an Italian economist, observed that 20 percent of the population owned 80 percent of the property in Italy. His discovery was later popularised by Joseph Juran, an engineer and one of the pioneers of modern quality management. Basically, Juran and Pareto realised that:

> *20 percent of our activities will generate 80 percent of our results, while the remaining 80 percent of our activities will only generate 20 percent of our results.*

Juran, looking at the idea from his quality improvement focus, noted that 80 percent of a problem is caused by 20 percent of the possible causes. (He didn't, however, suggest that we ignore the remaining 80 percent of the causes – he also talked about the 'vital few and the useful many'.)

Of course there are variations. Of course it doesn't hold true all the time. In some cases the ratios are 90/10 or 70/30. However, from the perspective of how we make time choices, it's a great filter.

Let's check some other ways we can apply these ratios to our lives and then we'll dig a bit deeper into how it applies to time.

EXAMPLES OF THE PARETO PRINCIPLE:
- If we own a business, typically 20 percent of our clients will be the source of 80 percent of our income. Conversely, 20 percent of our income will be generated by 80 percent of our clients. The same ratios usually apply to profit also.
- Take another look at the examples of Proactive activity above. And remember the definition – *anything that will make a positive long-term difference to my life.* Typical activities that fit into that quadrant are things that, if we engaged in them on a regular basis, would be 20 percenters making a long-term difference.
- Consider your wardrobe. You probably wear 20 percent of your clothes 80 percent of the time. (Unless you've just had a clean out!)
- Think of your garden, if you've got one. Let's say the flower beds are over-grown and the lawn looks like a hay field. Mowing the lawn will only take about 20 percent of your allocated gardening time yet will make 80 percent of the difference. If, on the other hand, you spend ages weeding the garden but ignore the lawn, any observer will glance at your property and think 'messy'.
- Now one for young parents. When I was a young mother the house was always messy. (Cut me some slack here, okay. Those six ankle-biters arrived in exactly nine years – to the day!) I didn't know some clever engineer had given it an equally clever Italian's name, but I applied the 80/20 rule every time I heard a car drive up my long drive. That first sound of a car grinding up the hill

gave me exactly four minutes before someone was knocking on my door. I can't tell you how many times baking dishes and pots were hidden in the oven. One day I even had to use the washing machine to stow the kitchen mess!

It constantly amazed me how much better the bombsite masquerading as our home looked with those dirty dishes out of sight, the sofa throw-over pulled up tidily and the worst of the toy mess picked up off the floor. Perhaps that's where I learnt to move quickly and deal with the most important things first!

So here's my 'grandma' advice to young parents: 20 percent of your precious time spent doing a surface tidy-up will generate 80 percent of the impact. Don't waste time being a perfectionist.

- This next example was shared by the Practise Manager of a regional accountancy firm. I met him whilst doing a national roadshow for the small business clients of a major bank.

Our biggest client was also our most difficult. They caused all manner of problems – constantly late with their documentation; slow payers; difficult to please; cranky and unpleasant people – and those were just a few of the challenges.

It reached the point that we were about to lose a couple of our top people, simply because they hated working with these clients so much. The management of the firm, rather anxiously, decided to invoke the 80/20 rule. Although these people were generating a significant amount of our income, they also created 80 percent of the hassle factor. We decided to 'fire' the client.

It was with some trepidation, hoping like heck that we were doing the right thing, that we told them we didn't now have the capacity to do their work.

Within a matter of days the atmosphere in our firm did a complete about-face. Suddenly everyone was happy again and the looming departures of our good people didn't eventuate. The 'spare' capacity created by the removal of such a large client was rapidly filled up with better-quality clients who appreciated us, got their documentation in on time and paid promptly. And – surprise,

---

> *surprise – the profitability of the firm also increased.*
>
> *It was the best thing we ever did.*

SO HOW DOES THIS PARETO PRINCIPLE HELP YOU PLAN YOUR TIME?

Imagine the impact if you spend 20 percent of your week (including those precious off-work hours) engaged in Proactive actions – activities that will make a long-term difference to your life.

Many people, especially those who work in very Reactive situations, or whose main activities are dictated by other people, may not be able to achieve this balance on a daily basis. However, if over a week you strive for 20 percent of Proactive action, 'magic' happens – and far faster than you ever thought possible. Perhaps you put some of this 20 percent into learning new skills in your own time and at your own cost. If your present employer doesn't recognise them, another will. Chances are very good that you'll end up with higher pay. At the very least it makes you more marketable or better qualified to start your own business.

> I want to support your commitment to getting a grip on your time challenges.
>
> Remember to download your extra bonus – our thank you for purchasing this book. You'll discover pearls of wisdom I've learnt from five of the world's top thought leaders on efficiency and productivity.
>
> Grab their wisdom with this **free** audio download http://gettingagrip.com/digitalgifts on how to make time for exercise, how to control your Inbox, practical advice on goals, simplicity, managing major projects and more.
>
> When you register to get your downloads you'll also receive a well-spaced supply of ongoing time tips and practical help. Should you wish to unsubscribe at any time, it's as easy as one click. We don't spam you and *never* share your details.

CHAPTER 5 DON'T SWEAT THE SMALL STUFF!

So now, let's consider how all this thinking ties together. It's time to study the technique of weekly planning.

SOME IMPORTANT POINTS ABOUT WEEKLY PLANNING

Let's consider the reasons behind weekly planning.

- **It links our goals to our actions**

  This is the best way I know to link our long-term goals with our day-to-day activities. It stops those exciting goals and Proactive plans from drifting like smoke into the blue yonder.

- **It gives us the best focus**

  When, in a beautiful garden we look closely at one plant, the rest of the garden will be slightly out of focus. If, instead, we stand back and take a wide-angle view of the whole garden we get a clearer perspective of shape, colour and layout.

  Scheduling our activities is no different. If we mainly focus on our daily task list we see clearly what's under our nose. It has its place but *be careful*. It tends to immerse us in the urgent, always trying to achieve more, faster, better. When the focus is on the Reactive tasks under our nose, including email and requests from other people, we can easily become caught in an addictive, tail-chasing trap.

  Instead, if we take responsibility for long-term results and plan our workload in a more strategic and Proactive way, even with work that others have requested from us, we put ourselves in the driving seat. We'll be far more able to achieve the things that really matter, we'll escape that life-quenching sensation of always being off the mark and it also dramatically increases our personal effectiveness.

- ## We're using our diary in the most effective way

Many people use their diary (calendar, scheduler, planner – it's the same thing) primarily to keep track of appointments. A lesser number also include notes and tasks or 'to-do' lists. These uses are good. They're certainly an advance on not using a diary at all. But – if this is all they're used for, their owners are missing the real power of the tool.

KEY POINT No. 13: *The people who get best value out of their diary use it as a* **Planning Tool,** *not just an appointment taker.*

HOW TO RUN YOUR WEEKLY PLAN

Whether you use an electronic system or a paper-based one it doesn't matter. The principles are the same and we discuss electronic calendars further in this chapter.

The next two graphics are a blank form and an example of the process we're about to discuss. You can also download a blank copy for your own use at http://links.gettingagrip.com/WeeklyPlanningSheet.pdf. (You'll notice it says 'Copyright'. Here's the deal – copy it right!)

Weekly planning sheet   WEEK ENDING _____
What is my focus for the week, in each activity area?

GOALS FOR WEEK		MONDAY	TUESDAY	WEDNESDAY	THURSDAY	FRIDAY	SATURDAY	SUNDAY
Self, Wellbeing & Spirit	7							
	8							
	9							
Business & Career	10							
	11							
	12							
	1							
Home & Family	2							
	3							
	4							
Community & Humanity	5							
	6							
	7							
	8							
© R. Pearce 1996 (2018)	9							

Weekly planning sheet.

Weekly planning sheet   WEEK ENDING _____
What is my focus for the week, in each activity area?

GOALS FOR WEEK		MONDAY	TUESDAY 6.30	WEDNESDAY	THURSDAY 6.30	FRIDAY	SATURDAY	SUNDAY
Self, Wellbeing & Spirit	7	Planning time! ↓	Gym ↓ 7.30		Gym ↓ 7.30			
Buy Think & Grow Rich & read 15 mins per day.	8						Gym ↓	
Gym x 3 per week	9		Call travel agent arrange w/end	Phone new potential clients	Individual staff meetings (6 x 30 mins)			
Business & Career	10	Suppliers' Meeting						
Book a management course.	11		Accountant – review systems ↓	Southern client visits				
Phone 5 potential new clients.	12	Buy Think & Grow Rich					Clean up tool shed	
Spend time with accountant reviewing our systems.	1	Brief Janet re training	↓		Lunch with Bob – discuss	Marketing meeting		
Home & Family	2				marketing ideas ↓			
Arrange a romantic weekend.	3				2.30			↓
Have a family scrabble night.						↓		
Clean up the tool shed.	4	Staff meeting ↓		↓				
Community & Humanity	5							
	6							
Ring Squash Club President re suggested security system.	7		Ph Squash Club Pres.		Scrabble night with children ↓		Dinner with Bob & Sue	
	8	Discuss w/end away with Phil		Squash club committee mtg. ↓				↓
© R. Pearce 1996 (2018)	9		↓					↓

Sample weekly planning sheet.

THE PLANNING PROCESS

1. Set about 15 minutes aside to plan the coming week.

2. Ensure that all the appointments and time-sensitive commitments you've already made are in your calendar. Don't proceed until this is done – it shows you how much time is available for Step 3.

3. Next is a mini goalsetting action that links to the earlier discussion in Chapter 3 about your Big Picture.

   Review your goals in each of the four main life areas:
   Self, Wellbeing and Spirituality
   Business and Career
   Home and Family
   Community and Humanity

   Consider which projects need some attention in the next week. In each area you wish to work on, identify one or two small goals for the coming week. Think especially about what Proactive activities you can include. It might be as small as a phone call to begin a project of long-term value. (It's now that the realistic, time-driven and specific SMART goalsetting becomes relevant.)

   If you're using my weekly planning page you've got space to write your goals in the left-hand column.

4. Now comes the step that turns your diary into a planning tool, not just an appointment taker. On your weekly plan, whether on paper or electronically, convert those small mini-goals into ***appointments with yourself***, in specific time slots. Allow plenty of non-allocated time between commitments; things always take longer than you think.

5. Now, when someone says *'Can I see you for a minute?'* (and of course it never takes just a minute!) make your first response a quick check of your diary. It's now that the wonderful power of that magic little word *'no'* kicks in. It might not be a flat *'no'*. It might instead be a negotiated alternative time. And of course sometimes you will choose to put aside what you'd previously planned and accept this new interruption. But, and this is the big *but* – at least you've taken that nano-second of thinking time to consider your priorities instead of blind acceptance of whatever comes at you.

SOME USEFUL FURTHER TIPS

- If you find that the day's urgencies wait to throttle you as you walk in the door at the beginning of the week, either plan at the end of the previous week or do it at home over the weekend. Or, become very good at making everything else wait for a few minutes on the first day of your week. If you don't do it *before* the week starts you'll probably never get to it. Some people like to plan on a Thursday afternoon. This gives them Friday to set up any necessary tasks, appointments or preparation.

- If the coming week is already full of activities and there's no space for even a few extra Proactive things, you might need to plan two or three weeks ahead in order to start changing from a Reactive to a more Proactive focus.

- Review what you've done or not done in the preceding week. Before you start Step 3 you may need to reschedule some items that remain from the week just completed. Also, notice what you have achieved and don't forget to give yourself credit for them. Too many people focus so much on the future and what they want to achieve that they forget to notice the successes of the 'now'.

- You may realise, as you review the previous week that you're trying to bite off more than you can chew. Success is achieving *something*, even if it's not as much as you want or had planned. Being realistic is the aim with weekly planning; it's better to tick off a few small Proactive tasks than aim too high and end up feeling demotivated. Steady, achievable and satisfying progress in all parts of your life is the objective. The only person holding the measuring stick is you, after all!
- Allow time for the unexpected. You're not trying to conquer the world in one week. You're in for the long haul. The trap that people often fall into after learning new information is that they try to take on too much and then give up in disappointment when they don't reach their objectives (which in fact were unrealistic!).
- Imagine, in twelve months' time, that you've only done half the Proactive things you'd wanted to do. Would you still have made significant progress in your life and with your long-term goals? Might you, in the past, have procrastinated on some of those activities?
- Many busy people realise, when they take an objective look at their lives, that they're short-changing themselves and their families of quality time. Their noses have been so glued to the grind-stone that they'd forgotten to look for better life balance. This then leads to less leisure time, longer work hours, more stress, more health problems and more broken relationships.
- If you use an electronic calendar system, the weekly planning process is easily integrated. Just set a recurring alert for your preferred planning slot. In the reminder you might like to add the four major life areas, with a note to self such as, '*What are my top one or two goals in each life area for the coming week?*'
- If you're using something like my Weekly Planning Sheet you might want to clip your weekly planning sheet into your meetings notebook, or a paper diary if you use one. Or it could be kept in the office in a special folder or on the wall.
- Some of my clients use the Weekly Planner to get a good overall view of the main events for the week and then transfer key and time-bound activities into their digital calendars. For the rest of the week they work off their electronic diaries.
- Many (including me) still prefer a paper diary. Don't stop, if that's

your preference. I love my smartphone and all the clever things I can do with it but I don't like the calendar view. It's slower when it comes to entering detailed information on my mobile and I can't see a full overview on the phone screen. However, I don't need to make my diary visible to others. (More on digital versus paper diaries in the next chapter.)

- If you must work with two diaries, make one the primary diary and try to have everything in it. When someone asks for an appointment, make the primary diary the *first* place to check – no exceptions. Otherwise things will inevitably fall through the cracks.
- This wide-view planning process can also be applied to a month; there's just less space to write. I now find, because I've internalised the 'big picture' focus so fully, that planning on a monthly basis is even faster and more effective, with just a quick review at the beginning of each week. However, for a long time I was very meticulous at detailed weekly planning. Until you've got the process well integrated, I do encourage you to do it weekly.

THE REAL WORK IS ALL DONE NOW!

Notice your feeling of control when you step back for a few minutes and become more objective. Keep up the practise until it becomes a habit to think from a weekly perspective. It really is quick, once you've mastered the technique. If, at some stage in the future you find yourself overwhelmed with too much to do, it will usually be because you've slipped up on this planning. Go back and start the habit again. You'll recapture that feeling of Proactive control. It's a more strategic way to look at your workload as well as your life.

CHAPTER 6 DAILY PLANNING AND DIARIES

The final step in *effective* use of our time is the way we make small choices throughout the day. The critical factor is learning to allocate some of the best part of your day to the things that *really* matter.

How often do you arrive at work with good intentions and an internal conversation going something like this?

'Today I am definitely going to start on that report for the boss. I'll book time with the new staff member to check how she's going. And that heap of professional journals isn't getting any smaller. Jim mentioned there was a very good article on paper-handling systems in one of them. I'm sick of my office looking like a bomb-site; I'll definitely dig that article out.'

But then something like the following happens:
You reach your office, the phone starts ringing, there's a pile of 'stuff' still waiting from yesterday and two staff members need to see you urgently. You plough straight into the fray, attending to each item as it waves its hand at you, much too busy to analyse what's going on. When the rush dies down it's 2p.m.

The good intentions have become rather jaded, your energy levels have dropped to survival mode because you've not taken time for lunch and you've just remembered that a newsletter must be done *now* or the secretary won't have time to finish it today.

You may find it reassuring to know that many other people operate the same way most of the time, but I'm not encouraging you to! Successful people don't make a regular habit of such work patterns. They don't just start with the tasks under their nose or the ones making the most noise. They don't get distracted by all the interesting or easier items that gobble up huge tracts of time. Of course, it's more fun doing the easy and obvious things and appeals to our sense of instant gratification. But, if we're really honest with ourselves, some of these items can usually either wait, be passed on to someone else or don't really need to be done.

THE TINY INVESTMENT THAT SAVES HOURS

Daily planning is simple and very quick – *if* we've already done our planning for the week. Think of it as an investment – of time.

1. Review the already-scheduled appointments. This is an opportunity for adjustment if something urgent has swooped in.
2. Do a quick reality check on the list of tasks you'd hoped to achieve. What is *really* likely to fit into today's gaps? Because we've already done our major wide-angle strategic focus for the week it becomes much easier to defer the time-stealers that don't really matter, or make adjustments if necessary.
3. Apply Ivy Lee's technique as described next.
4. Feel the satisfaction as you control your day's activities better.

IVY LEE'S DAILY 1–5 LIST

This famous legend beautifully illustrates a very simple daily planning method. I believe it was the source of the complicated ABC and numeric prioritising described earlier in the book.

In America in the early 1900's the head of Bethlehem Steel, Charles Schwab, called in his public relations consultant Ivy Lee (who also had an interest in business productivity) to suggest ways to make Bethlehem Steel more effective.

Here's my interpretation of the simple process Mr Lee recommended:

- At the beginning of the day (or the night before), make a list of all the things you want to do for the day, in no particular order.
- Then identify the top five activities. Number them 1 through 5, wherever they are on the list. Don't bother to number the rest of the list – just the top five.
- Start at No. 1 and don't go off it until you've finished, gone as far as you wish to go, or as far as you're able to go.
- When interruptions come, as they always do, ask yourself: *'Is this new activity more important than the one I'm working on?'*

If it's not, add the new thing to your list, put it out of eye-range so it doesn't distract you and stay focused on the more important activity. However, if it *is* more important, put the other task aside, work on the new job and when completed go back to your list (which has been considered and thought about before the day started bossing you around!).

- Each time you move to the next number down, check the list. If something that's jumped on the list during the day is of higher priority than the activity you'd planned to do, give it lead position. Because the other things are written on the list instead of jostling for mind space you can keep them under tight rein – they won't distract you.
- If there's any day left once the top five and any relevant queue jumpers have been handled, go back to the list and number off another five. This saves time at the beginning of the day prioritising things that you may never get to.
- If, at the end of the day you've only done the first one or two items and everything else was a queue-jumper, at least you have the satisfaction of going home knowing that you've done the most important tasks for the day.

When Schwab asked how much he wished to be paid for this wisdom, Lee answered, '*Teach it to your managers, all use it for a month and then pay me what you think it's worth.*'

A month later a cheque for US$25,000 landed on Ivy Lee's desk. (That's a lot of money even today! Think of the value about 100 years ago!)

When asked later why he paid so much for such seemingly simple information, Mr Schwab replied that it was the single most useful piece of advice he had ever received and significant in moving Bethlehem Steel into the pre-eminent position in the steel industry that it subsequently enjoyed.

Keep your daily planning simple and flexible.

KEY POINT No. 14: *It's really simple to take control of your time – just begin the day with the most important tasks, including something of longer-term value if at all possible. Even 30 minutes on a long-term*

task makes a difference, not only to your productivity but also to how you feel.

MORE USEFUL TIPS FOR DAILY PLANNING

- Interruptions are easier to handle when we work from the top of our priority list. Partly this is because our self-esteem is higher when we control at least some of our actions by *choosing* to put higher value actions at the top of our list. Even if major crises erupt we still have a feeling of control. The alternative is to let a miscellany of random events and other people's priorities push us around.
- Once the top priority things are handled, the rest of the day usually flows very easily.
- If we've already done our weekly planning we're one step ahead of Ivy Lee's process, for some of our top items are already scheduled into the week as appointments. A daily list becomes the prioritising of everything else.
- No item shares the same value, because although we can simultaneously do a couple of simple things, like hold for a caller and continue typing, we can only hold one thought in our mind at a time. There may be many equally important things on your list but – you have to make a choice. This simple process unclogs our mind. Multi-tasking is hazardous and mostly leads to inefficiency. Read more about that in Chapter 7.
- Chunk similar activities together. For example: a chunk of email time, a batch of calls, some filing or a set time on data entry. It's more efficient to do 'like' activities at the same time.
- Caution – don't plan too tightly. 'Stuff' will always happen, so leave some space in your day.

KEY POINT No. 15: *Successful people DON'T start with the easy things. Instead, they begin with the most important tasks – and that is very rarely email.*

DIARIES

Rather than recommend a particular system I've focused on giving you the principles and concepts to help you choose what suits you best, or adapt something to your way of working. One thing I've learnt over my many years in this field is that there is no one 'right way'.

PAPER-BASED OR ELECTRONIC?

There are very good reasons to have everyone in a company all using electronic systems that everyone can access and we'll discuss that in a minute. However, there is something quite important and little understood that needs to be covered first.

Your preference will be impacted by the way you like to capture, process and memorise information.

We have five possible different ways of processing and retaining information:
- Visual
- Auditory
- Kinaesthetic (tactile)
- Olfactory (smell)
- Gustatory (taste)

Although the last two are very powerful at a profoundly deep level it's the first three that, for almost everyone, will have the greatest impact on our preferences about how to work efficiently.

For instance:
- A visual processor likes to *see* things quickly. They love whiteboards, wall charts, anything they can see at a glance. Once they see something they find it easy to remember. Give them colour, pictures, visually pleasing equipment and environments and they're happy campers. Some visuals don't like smartphone calendars because they can't quickly see both the details and the overall picture. Also, they like attractive-looking planners and journals, of which there are many.
- Auditory processors divide into two sub-categories – auditory tonal (sound) and auditory digital (making logic and meaning by writing things down). The tonal people remember by *hearing*. Once heard, seldom forgotten. The digital people are the list-makers, the ones who find clarity and better recall by *writing down what they hear*. Not all auditory digitals like electronic

diary systems. Especially if they're fast touch typists, the peck-and-hunt technique of the tiny screens is frustratingly fiddly.

- And then there are the kinaesthetic processors. Many tactile folk love a paper-based physical diary – they have to *feel* connected to their life. They prefer to hold a pen or pencil in their hand. They also enjoy the sensory experience of a good-feeling cover – leather, soft cloth or some kind of texture. It's a tangible anchor to their priorities.

Now digital calendars have become a standard business tool, an interesting trend is appearing. A research study was done by Get Control, a company that specialises in teaching computer skills. In their sample they found that 78 percent of people of all ages have *returned* to paper diaries/journals as their primary planning tool and to-do lists. This is rarely because they're resistant-to-technology Luddites. They might be using their electronic calendars for key appointments, but they found that a total digital reliance slowed them down and didn't give the same fast and easy overview.

And it's nothing to do with age – even digital natives (people born since the widespread use of digital technology) and people working in very high-tech environments are to be seen with pencil or pen and paper as their thinking and planning devices. Neuro-scientists tell us there's a higher connectivity between the action of writing with a pen or pencil and our short-term memory retention and understanding, than if we just use a keyboard. Test it for yourself.

There are many kinds of paper diaries available. Look for them well before the end of the year. I like to view them in person so I can make sure they meet my needs. When I had to change brands because my favourite became unavailable I took longer to choose a diary than a dress!

If you have only a small number of commitments, a simple 1-page-per-day diary in conjunction with my weekly planner may be all you need. Did you download a sample? Here's the link again http://links.gettingagrip.com/WeeklyPlanningSheet.pdf. Or maybe just the weekly planner itself is sufficient for your needs if your life is very uncluttered.

Caution: Just because a diary looks nice doesn't mean it's effective.

Those with multiple sections appear to have lots of flexibility and choice of where to write things, but too many options are confusing. If you find yourself unsure where you should write something, there are three possibilities:

1. The system isn't right for your way of processing information.
2. You haven't been given enough instruction how to use it.
3. It hasn't been designed from a good time management perspective.

MULTIPLE DIARIES

Unless you need a desk diary at your office for staff to record client appointments, don't fall into the trap of running several diary or calendar systems – you only create confusion and extra work trying to keep them all up to date.

If you've got a secretary or assistant (or you are the secretary and need to manage your boss) there are a couple of ways to efficiently and jointly manage a diary:

1. Agree which parts of the week are your responsibility and which are under the control of the other person. Then if someone wants to make an appointment in the part of the week controlled by your colleague, you'll say, *'I'll need to get back to you to confirm this slot.'*
2. Allow the secretary to manage the entire appointment schedule. Ask anyone who wants to meet with you to contact the secretary. He or she will post the appointment in calendar. The next synchronisation (either manually or electronically) will update whatever system the diary owner uses.

   Example. A business owner I know prefers a very small pocket system because he's frequently out of the office and offline. His secretary does all his bookings and flicks him a quick email to update. It's a tiny bit of double-handling but works very effectively for them.

There is no one right way to manage our planning methods. Find the way that works best for you and be prepared to adapt someone else's system if necessary.

TIPS TO MANAGE ELECTRONIC DIARIES

If you love your electronic diary or you're in a large organisation that uses an electronic calendar as a communal scheduling system, make sure your major Proactive activities are there, not just meetings.

Even if you plan the week on paper, take a few minutes to transfer key activities into the digital calendar. Although it might be a small amount of double-handling there are numerous time-saving advantages.

1. Anyone needing to set a meeting can see everyone's availabilities in a few keystrokes, rather than wasting time with phone calls or emails as they try to diary-match.
2. Especially in an environment that uses electronic diaries, it's critical that you block out your 'appointments with yourself'. Unless you've given permission to another user, no-one can see what you're doing but they can see that you're not available. If you don't do this simple step, you'll find yourself pushed and pulled by everyone else's finger-tips!
3. Recurring activities can be set in seconds. This can save a lot of time.
4. You can also click and drag an email into your calendar, saving re-writing. (See Chapter 10 for more on using your email system efficiently.)

KEY POINT No. 16: *There's no one right way to do anything. Modify the systems others recommend to suit your own way of working and unique circumstances.*

ONE FINAL MATTER – STAY WITH THE PROGRAMME!

Self-discipline, as we discussed at the beginning of the book, is the key element in developing and maintaining a good planning habit. I **guarantee** you amazing results if you stick with your daily and weekly planning until it becomes a habit.

There's a very fine line between successful people and those who struggle. Everyone has the same amount of time. Successful people just use their time more powerfully and productively. The others don't have a clear picture of where they're headed, they lack a clear definite purpose and a vision of their possibilities, or they've either not learnt or haven't applied the principles we've just discussed.

The principles work – will you? A day at a time, let's use this gift of life to the full.

KEY POINT No. 17: *Constantly ask yourself: What is the best use of my time right now?*

A PRAYER FOR TODAY

This is the beginning of a new day.
God has given me this day to use as I will.
I can waste it... or use it for good
but what I do today is important
because I am exchanging a day of my life for it!

When tomorrow comes this day will be gone forever,
leaving in its place something that I have traded for it.
I want it to be gain and not loss;
good and not evil;
success and not failure;
in order that I shall not regret the price I have paid for it.

(Author unknown)

PART TWO

NOW WE'VE SORTED THE FOUNDATIONS, LET'S LOOK AT EVERYTHING ELSE

CHAPTER 7 TIPS AND TECHNIQUES

Dost thou love life? Then do not squander time;
for that's the stuff life is made of.
(Benjamin Franklin)

In Part One we discussed the first two elements of the Toolbar of Time – the importance of *clarity* and *focus* through having clear goals, then how to be *effective* – at putting our energy into the activities which will make a long-term difference. Now your foundations are laid we can focus on the tips and techniques, the practical efficiencies that streamline our work habits and make us more *efficient*.

In this chapter we're going to:
- identify most of the major time-wasters.
- discuss ways to beat them.
- learn how to focus on Proactive rather than Reactive activities.

MAJOR TIME-WASTERS
1. Interruptions
2. Multi-tasking
3. Email and social media
4. Telephones
5. Open plan offices
6. Visitors, drop-in colleagues and the open-door policy
7. Paper
8. Lack of planning
9. Fire-fighting
10. Socialising
11. Indecision
12. Perfectionism
13. Screen time

A few chapters back we discussed the 80/20 rule. To recap, 80 percent of the highest priority tasks for the day can usually be achieved in about 20 percent of the time you have available. So, what's happening during the rest of the day? How much time can we save by looking at *how* we do *what* we do?

Time-wasters wave at us all day long. In our heart of hearts we know what they are. Often we think there's nothing we can do. In fact, there's always a solution, if we bend our mind enough to seek it. The best tool to fight them is a firm decision to concentrate on the few things that, in a day, will make a long-term difference. Then those sneaky time-stealers don't get as much chance to wreak havoc on your schedule. If we don't have this focus it's very easy to slip into Time-wasting mode.

Many people are happy to hang comfortably on to the shirt-tails of their old habits, to stay in their comfort zone. They're uncomfortable about standing out from the mass and would rather carry on the Time-wasting habits of their associates. I don't think that sort of person is reading this book!

Top achievers don't waste time and are prepared to be seen as leaders in their field. Sometimes, when you first start learning about principles of effective living, it seems a lonely walk but, if you persevere, it very quickly becomes richly satisfying. On the way you meet many other successful people with a similar outlook.

INTERRUPTIONS

When I wrote the first edition of this book we didn't have interruptions as a separate category, but now we have to contend with the dramatic increase in digital interferences of email, smartphones and other devices. Add the big increase in open plan workspaces and it's no wonder interruptions have become pandemic. (Many of the tips that follow also fit in the general category of interruptions, but for ease of use I've broken them into separate topics.)

A few years ago I interviewed Jonathan Spira, the author of *Overload! How Too Much Information Is Hazardous To Your Organization.* He's also a founding member of IORG, the Information Overload Research Group and has spent many years researching the impact of the knowledge economy on some of the world's top companies.

Most of Spira's book discusses the seriousness of information overload in the digital environment and gives strategies to solve it. Email is top of the list, which is ironic, given that it's supposed to make our business dealings more efficient. (Read his observations on some of the causes of the 2007-8 global financial crisis and what also happened in the US Army and you'll query that efficiency.) His book was published in 2011 – I suspect he'd include notifications from phone apps to the top billing with email if he were to re-edit it.

If you'd like more information on this very serious problem, plus his eight ways to take control, grab yourself a copy of his excellent book.

He had this to say:

> *Interruptions plus recovery time consume as much as 28 percent of an average knowledge worker's day. In an average day that's 2.1 hours a day.*
>
> *On average the recovery time is **10-20 times the length of the interruption**. A 30-second interruption can result in as much as 5 minutes of recovery time. In some cases, the knowledge worker never returns to the original task and when and if it's restarted later, the penalty (i.e. recovery time) is far greater.*
>
> *Each time an individual switches tasks and tries to return to the previous task he has to go back in time, recollect his thoughts and recall exactly what he has done and what he has yet to do. Some repetitive work may be involved as well (e.g. redoing the last few steps.) This of course assumes that the individual returns at all – in some instances, the task is forgotten altogether. The interruptions also increase the likelihood of errors being committed.*
>
> *The other critical factor is how long it takes to get back into flow once you do start a task again. If it has any degree of complexity, it will generally take about 15-20 minutes. In many open-plan environments, workers never get that much uninterrupted time.*

My 'in-the-field' observation is that, as the digital world becomes more entrenched, the lost time for many workers is now higher than 28 percent. And we wonder why people have to come in early or stay late to get the real work done!

Interruptions come in many guises – phone calls, texts or instant messages, any smartphone app alerts you've allowed, colleagues, self-interruptions ...and more. But as Jonathan highlighted, it's the digital interruptions that are the most invasive and addictive. They've changed the landscape profoundly, in our personal as well as our business lives. It's only when I look at the first edition of this book that I fully appreciate how different; the changes have sneaked up on us year on year. These days it seems that people can't or won't go anywhere without their smartphones – and I include myself in that group. We've become so reliant on them that we carry interruptions with us wherever we go – *if we allow them.*

MULTI-TASKING

As a woman, I used to smile complacently when multi-tasking was mentioned. If it was a group of women talking, there'd be little quips such as, *'We know guys can't think of more than one thing at a time. Ask them something really important when they're watching TV and you'll never get an intelligent answer.'*

But guys, you have the last laugh. There is now a heap of research to show that constant multi-tasking is not so smart – and I've participated in some of it.

Perhaps women can cope a little better than men. But – it's not smart to even try. Both genders get frazzled, exhausted and frustrated when they've got too many things going on at the same time. And they lose hours in a day.

So – go the people who stay focused on one thing at a time! Keep it up. You'll get your work done faster than your multi-tasking colleagues.

Why? Further to the information from Jonathan and the time taken in *switching* from task to task, another issue is the number of times we *don't* get back to the previous task, sometimes for hours, sometimes never. Once our train of thought is broken it takes a lot more mental energy to return.

Don't believe me? How many open emails and applications do you have on your computer right now? How many items of paper or equipment are in your immediate space, waiting for you to decide where to put them? What actions or activities are awaiting a final decision or completion?

And what happens when we live constantly in a world where everything goes at warp speed, with multiple distractions? Think of many modern offices. There's constant low-level (or sometimes high-level) noise and movement. Phones ring, people walk by, emails ping as they arrive and conversations happen all around you.

My friend and associate Steuart Snooks in Melbourne, who specialises in helping people conquer email overload, had this to say about multiple distractions: *'A common result is pseudo ADD, a term coined by two Harvard psychology professors to explain addiction to the bombardment of information. They've noticed that many people experience shortened attention span because of the forms of communications used today. This has a sustained negative neurological effect as well. It isn't an illness; it's purely a response to the hyper-kinetic environment in which we live.*

'So, when a manager is desperately trying to deal with more than he can possibly handle, the brain and body get locked into a circle where the brain's frontal lobes lose their sophistication. We get black and white thinking and we start to lose perspective and shades of grey. People with this sort of difficulty struggle to stay organised, to set priorities and to manage their time. They experience a constant low-level feeling of panic and guilt.'

I recommend you download his free report *The 7 Critical Impacts of Information & E-mail Overload.*

Paul Chin, another commentator in this issue of information overload, says, *'Rampant multi-tasking and the deluge of available information has ... created a paradox. The more we try to do, the less we get done. And the more inundated we are with information the less time we spend absorbing it.'*

EMAIL AND APPS

We'll go into much more depth on email techniques in Chapters 10 and 11 on email and paper management. For now I'll just mention two top-level time-savers.

1. Turn off the alerts on your computer and phone. Very few of us need to know we've just received mail or yet another Facebook notification. Why? Re-read the section above on interruptions.
2. Don't do email first thing in the day. (Don't hit me – the explanation is in Chapter 10!)

TELEPHONE TIPS FOR BUSINESS CALLS

- Learn to control the telephone, or it will control you.
- Aim for quick, to-the-point conversations.
- Don't get bogged down in social chit-chat during work time.

Notice how you start and finish business conversations. Do you say *'How are you?'* instead of *'How can I help you?'* Ever heard yourself, at the end of a conversation, say things like *'How was your holiday?'* Or *'What are you doing for the weekend?'* and then wished, ten minutes later, that you hadn't?

If you are the caller, get to the point immediately by saying, *'The purpose of my call is ...'*. The person at the other end immediately knows that you respect their time.

If a caller is long-winded, here are a few suggestions:

- Create a sense of urgency by using phrases such as *'I know you're busy, so I won't hold you up'*, *'Before we finish, the last point is ...'* or if it's a friend *'I know I can't take up your work time on personal chat. Let's get together after work sometime.'*

- If you've finished the business and the caller has verbal diarrhoea, a tongue-in-cheek solution is to cut yourself off.

- If you're desperate but too kind to be blunt, drop something noisy onto the floor and say *'I'm sorry, something's fallen over. I'll have to go.'*
- If on a mobile phone: *'The battery's running down. I'll have to finish very soon.'* (Well, it is running down if it's being used, isn't it?)

Sometimes the hardest person to train is yourself. Try an egg-timer on your desk and flip to start when you pick up the phone. It might help you develop a sense of urgency.

Make a mini-agenda in your diary or journal before placing a call, especially if you have more than one thing to discuss. How many times have you had several topics to cover, not written them down and then wasted time trying to remember? Or, someone has called back hours after you've left a message and you hear yourself say *'I know there's something else I wanted to talk about.'* Isn't it frustrating! I've fallen into that trap more than once!

If your job requires very solid concentration, such as computer programming or an in-depth and complex report, taking a phone call could cost you up to two hours of wasted work because of the time needed to re-focus. You would think people wouldn't take calls when in full concentration mode, but not necessarily so! If you need that degree of focus, let calls go to voicemail until you're ready. It's your electronic secretary.

If you'd lose customers if the phone isn't answered by a real person, consider a paging service. Being 100 percent available is *not* the answer.

Batch or chunk your calls. If you return a bunch of calls all at the same time, you'll find you take much less time than if you'd answered each one as it came in. You create a sense of urgency, which helps you action the calls much more quickly. Incoming calls haven't broken your concentration. The same strategy applies to making out-going calls.

Phone calls during meetings

- If someone has made an appointment to see you, it's very discourteous to respond to the phone. The one who has invested time to come to your office deserves top priority. Taking the phone call also disrupts your focus, causing the appointment to take longer than necessary.

- Have your calls held by the receptionist or secretary if you have one, send the call to voice mail or turn the phone off.
- These points apply to staff members as well as external visitors. Consider the lost opportunity cost to the company of having a staff member twiddling their thumbs while you take yet another call!
- If you have a colleague who constantly keeps you waiting while they take calls, walk out of the room (but use with caution if it might be career-limiting!). You may need to leave them a note as to when you'll next be available. Or, perhaps you could say *'Shall I ask the receptionist to hold calls for us both?'* (if calls come from a switchboard.)
- If your mobile must be answered, or you're waiting for a really critical call, ask a colleague to mind your phone and only interrupt you if absolutely essential.
- If you're working on-site at a client's premises, be quick if you must take a call. When someone is paying for your time, they don't want you to be interrupted by outside calls on their dime.

OPEN PLAN OFFICES

Many people do not work as efficiently in constant close quarters with other people. If this is you, look for quieter places when you need to concentrate. If you're aware of the conditions in which you work best, it would also be a good idea to try and avoid employment situations that you know will put you under stress.

Is it possible to do some of your work at home, away from distractions? Perhaps you don't mind some noise, but struggle with your colleagues' *'do you have a minute?'* requests. You might prefer a café. The anonymous chatter of unknown people gives a background hum but people aren't interrupting you constantly. And what about working flexi-time?

Tess was Events Manager for a small family-owned publishing firm that specialised in the tourist market. She made a lot of phone calls to clients and prospects.

In a training session the conversation turned to office layout, noise, distractions and efficiency. We discussed the working preferences of the members of the team and several commented that they were distracted by noise. Then Tess chipped in.

'You guys know I found the noise in the big office difficult.' (Most of the staff worked in a large open-plan office.)

'Since I moved into my tiny office' (jokes started flying about Tess's 'cupboard') *'I achieve the same amount of work in four days that I used to do in five.'*

Dramatic as Tess's story is, I've heard variations of it ever since I began this work in the early 90s. The thing is, for every worker who struggles to work well in an open plan office, there's a largely invisible waste of company resources. Yes, there are benefits. But is it really a cost-saver? How many decision-makers and designers, when planning a new office layout, take into account the lost opportunity cost of interruptions?

Am I saying open plan layouts are all bad? No. But I am saying that they need managing if you're to have any hope of reasonable efficiency in this heavily interruption-prone environment. There's an increasing body of research showing that the supposed benefits are fraught with pitfalls.

If open plan layout is a productivity drain in your organisation, check the following simple strategies. (You'll find each of them expanded in *Getting a Grip on the Paper War.)*

- **Quiet rooms** – with a computer terminal and/or a plug for your laptop.
- **Headsets.** An increasingly popular solution to distractions from other people's conversation is to wear headphones when concentrating, with or without music. It gives a visual message to others that you do not wish to be disturbed. Some managers worry about poor collegiality; as long as they're not used to the

point that people can't communicate with the wearer, I consider head-sets to be a great option.

Aside from blocking noise, researcher Dr David Lewis, founder of Mindlab International, found that nine out of ten workers performed better when listening to music. What sort depends on the work you're doing *and your learning style*. One expert suggests the following guidelines:

» Pop music when you're doing data entry, spell-checking or anything that requires fast action.
» Classical music if you're working on numbers or need attention to detail.
» Ambient music if your work involves solving equations – it's easy to ignore.
» Dance music if proof-reading and problem-solving. (I certainly couldn't do proofing to dance music! I'd find it way too distracting, but it might work for you.)

- **Red Time or Power Hour.** This is a period of the day when no-one is allowed to interrupt you. The rest of the time you can take interruptions, even though you're busy. Create a signal that your colleagues recognise. The signal or symbol sends a silent visual message that you're not available (as long as team members are educated to take the issue seriously).
- **Shut the door** (if you have one) for **at least** an hour a day and allow no interruptions. This is an extension of the Red Time/ Power Hour strategy.
- **Work from home** some of the time, or somewhere off-site – as discussed above.
- **Hot desks.** This is becoming fashionable in large firms with expensive CBD floor space. People who spend a lot of time out of office, e.g. sales reps or consultants, don't need a fully dedicated office. Instead, they bring their files and laptop with them whenever they need to be at the office.

Some companies have roll-out desks which are folded up and parked in storage whilst the owner is offsite. In some cases the mobile worker books space; in other companies there are enough free spaces for whoever needs them. Typically, a mobile workspace is only a small desk, power and an intranet connection or wireless capability. A second screen to link to the laptop is an efficient extra tool if possible.

When each user leaves they take their personal items, leaving the space free for the next occupant.

VISITORS, DROP-IN COLLEAGUES AND THE OPEN-DOOR POLICY

Of course, a lot of highly important work requires you to talk to people. The tips I'm now going to discuss may help you to be Proactive rather than Reactive.

Do you actually enjoy having people drop in? Could you do it elsewhere? Have meetings outside the workplace. Suggest lunch, or a coffee somewhere else. It's more refreshing, you're not interrupting colleagues and you'll probably find you come back more focused to work.

A complete open-door policy, which has been a popular management technique for some years, is not conducive to good time handling. Popular business practise has gone too far down the *I must be always there for my people* philosophy, to the point that many managers feel as though all they do is everybody else's work instead of their own. Result? They go home either exhausted from over-work and ridiculous hours or frustrated because they were so busy helping everyone else that they never got their own work done.

When faced with *'Have you got a minute?'* don't fall into the courtesy trap of saying *yes* when it's really a *no*. Learn to give a polite *no* but tell them when they *can* see you. If your staff are used to you dropping everything whenever they put their head around your door or rock up at your desk, you might have to re-educate them. They'll be pleased with the improved efficiency once they get used to the new regime. One benefit is that at least half the problems they think they need your help on will be solved before you're ready for them, once you teach them to think before they come. Plus, you're setting a good example about how to handle questions and interruptions.

As long as the staff have been properly trained (more on this in Chapter 9 on Delegation) they don't need to be constantly spoon-fed. It's also better usage of time for their managers to have periods of the day when they can work uninterrupted for at least one or two hours. Some managers find it hard to accept that they are not indispensable, but they only delude themselves. As Michael Gerber says throughout his best-selling business management book *The E Myth Revisited: why most small businesses don't work and what to do about it*, a successful company is able to run effectively without the boss always present.

KEY POINT No. 18: *We educate the people around us how to treat us.*

Here are some strategies if you see a long-winded visitor coming and you don't want them to settle in for a long chat.

- Rise to your feet as they approach (as if you were about to leave your desk on an errand). If they sit down, it's often much harder to dislodge them.
- If it was appropriate for them to sit down but now you want to bring the discussion to a close, stand up.
- Let the visitor see you looking at your watch. Say, *'I'm sorry, I will have to finish this meeting in ... minutes. I have another appointment.'* Even if the appointment is with yourself, it's still true.
- Walk a visitor to the door, saying, *'I'll walk with you out to reception. I have to see ...'*, or *'I'll discuss this last point as I come with you to the lift.'*
- If you regularly have unwelcome visitors who don't get the hint, remove any spare chairs.
- If necessary, don't make eye-contact with the chatty one. Keep your head down and continue working. Say something like *'I'm sorry I haven't time to stop just now. I've got a tight schedule on this one.'*
- Perhaps the would-be visitor is lonely or unhappy. What about scheduling a time to get together, outside of work time, and give them your full attention? They might just need a friend, but don't know how to ask.
- Shut the door if you have one and if necessary put up a *Do Not*

Disturb sign. One funny sign I spotted says *'I'm in here. You're out there. Let's keep it that way a while longer.'*

- If you're in an open-plan office, have a signal on your desk that your colleagues recognise, or a humorous sign on the back of your chair. For example, *'Beware, brain at work'* or some message that visitors can readily interpret as *'Quiet needed, thanks'*.
- If you have a secretary, lucky you. A good secretary will anticipate your needs. Ask him or her to interrupt you with a reminder about an imaginary appointment if a visitor has been with you longer than a pre-arranged time.
- If you have to share office space and you find other people's visitors distract you, constructive conversation with your office buddy is the first step. Maybe they don't realise how disruptive you find it. Instead of using 'you' language such as *'Your visitors talk too loudly, or too long'* try 'I' language, e.g. *'I wonder if you could help me. I have a challenge with being able to concentrate when some of your visitors come in. Any ideas about how we can find a solution that suits everyone?'*
- In discussions about problems, always look for a way to take responsibility. It disarms the other person. You give them emotional and mental space to be able to hear what you're saying. When we feel accused or blamed we are psychologically incapable of anything except defence; our natural response is to either attack in return or defend our position.

PAPER

The idea of a paperless office was first introduced by IBM in 1975. Although many of us are printing less since the advent of reliable cloud storage and fast internet, I don't foresee a completely paperless world any time soon. This is a big topic so we'll cover it comprehensively in Chapter 11.

LACK OF PLANNING

This is another very popular time stealer. Think back to the last time you *didn't* plan something properly and tried to wing it. Sometimes it works, but isn't there generally a nagging thought at the back of your mind that if you'd been better prepared you would have had a better outcome?

The people who don't plan their day have two common conversations. Most will say they haven't got time to do it; a few don't see the need. Planning takes time but saves time in the end.

Sometimes when people hear what kind of work I do, they launch into justification. I remember a printer saying defensively, *'I haven't got time to worry about planning. There's just too much going on, and it all has to be done. Time management – that's for other people.'* I doubt if she's still in business. You could see the stress and tension written all over her. She certainly hadn't spent any significant time in Proactive activities; her life was obviously very pressured, swinging madly between Frenetic and Reactive. No point in winning the battle, if you lose the war. To put it another way – what value is daily accomplishment if you lose your health, your family and your peace of mind? When we take time to step back and take an objective view of what's going on, there are always other ways of doing things.

Others *think* planning is a good idea but for one reason or another aren't doing it. Maybe you can identify with a woman in one of my classes who exclaimed in shock, *'I used to do this stuff, and it* really *worked! Why did I stop?'* She'd merely fallen out of the habit and only needed a reminder.

Some of the participants in a training session were giving me excuses as to why, one week after our first session (which had focused on the planning techniques we discussed earlier) they had not done their weekly planning. They were all senior executives. One of their group, a very organised and efficient man, quietly said *'I've used a similar system for a long time. I used to have trouble also, but I made myself stick to the practise of this planning stuff. I assure you that I could not achieve anything like as much as I do if I hadn't persevered. It wasn't always easy, but the effort has been rewarded many times over. The hardest bit was the thinking about it!'*

And then there are the folks who've never known how. Just reading a book once won't make you good at managing your time. You have to practise, practise, practise, make mistakes and start over again.

It doesn't matter if you stuff up. So does everyone. What makes a difference is what you do next. Winners learn from their mistakes, self-correct and then get back to the discipline of one day at a time practising the necessary habits. As I mentioned at the beginning, I used to be very bad at time management, so bad that I went on lots of courses and read many books in an effort to drag myself out of the mire. It took me some years to self-correct my poor time habits and even still I occasionally let myself down. But what I found worked well was to acknowledge my mistakes, evaluate what could have been done better and move on with a positive expectation of success. Nothing is ever gained by beating up on ourselves and giving up on new habits we're learning.

KEY POINT No. 19: *If you stuff up, just have another go. Success comes to those who persist.*

Bonus planning tips for the chronically late

If you're constantly challenged to get places on time and your friends and family say *'He's never on time'* or *'Doesn't she know how to organise herself?'*, try these three simple tricks. (I expand on them in Tips 38 and 39 of *About Time − 120 time-saving tips for those with no time*.)

1. If, as you're about to head out the door or leave your desk, you habitually think to yourself, *'I'll just do that one last* thing' – don't! One last email, that urgent phone call, the washing you'll just hang out before you leave for work – they're *guaranteed* to make you late.

2. Get ready first. Prepare at the beginning of the day for everything you have to do that day. Then go on with your work, setting an alert to give you 15 – 20 minutes' notice that it's time to leave for the next activity. There'll be no rushing around gathering things at the last minute. Instead, you'll delight in walking calmly out the door in good time.

3. When you have to go somewhere, start with the end in mind. Chronically late people don't do this; organised folks do it so naturally they can't understand why everyone else doesn't. Count back approximately how many minutes you need for each step of the way, until you arrive at the beginning. A chronically late person will typically say to themselves, *'That's ridiculously*

early. I'll be sitting around waiting!' You won't, you know. You'll just be less stressed. But always take a useful task to do on arrival, just in case.

KEY POINT No. 20: *By failing to plan you're planning to fail. (An oldie but a goodie!)*

FIRE-FIGHTING

If you've done your planning and spent some regular time on Proactive activities, you should only have a few crises. The best way to avert a crisis is anticipate it. If the same situation arises again, there's probably no clear policy or process to deal with it.

- Take time to think. Don't rush in until you've considered the possibilities and options open to you.
- Ask questions. What's the real problem? Where possible, get input from more than one source.
- What can you ask others to help with? Don't try and be Superman/ Woman, solving all the problems singlehandedly.
- Once you've made a decision, get on with it. She who hesitates is lost!
- What can be done to avoid the same problem happening again?

Common reasons for crises are:
- Lack of planning.
- Unrealistic time frames.
- Problem-orientation instead of opportunity-orientation.
- A reluctance by subordinates to break bad news, perhaps because they don't know that you really need a rapid flow of information, or because you've bitten their head off in the past.

SOCIALISING

Up to 30 percent of some employees' time is wasted socialising. In my very early days in real estate I was one of them; it was great fun taking long boozy lunches with the men I worked with. Then I began to notice that the staff who took very extended tea-breaks, regular social lunch-breaks and lots of chats in the corridors were the ones who made the least money.

If you're self-employed or on commission, a useful question might be: *'How much am I earning while I socialise?'* If you're on salary or wages sometimes ask yourself, *'Am I giving my best value to my company?'* The over-riding question for us all is, *'What is the most valuable use of my time, right now?'* As I became more confident in my work I realised that I enjoyed my socialising more when I'd done a good week's work. Having fun outside of work hours became a more satisfying norm. Outcomes: more money, (if you're self- employed) or happier employers if in a job.

Think of yourself as self-employed and head of your own corporation. If you receive a salary from someone, they are just your No. 1 client. As we take responsibility for ourselves and develop a self-directed attitude, we find ourselves looking for opportunities for advancement instead of passively accepting what life (and the boss) dish out.

INDECISION

Most indecision is caused by ignorance, fear, or lack of confidence in the facts. Improve your fact-finding procedures and learn to listen to your intuition.

Helpful decision-making questions:

- What result do we want?
- What benefits are there in each of the possible options?
- What can go wrong?
- What other ways are there of achieving the same result?
- What other information do I need before I can make this decision?
- Who do I need to speak to?
- What is my gut instinct here?

Still confused? A very easy way to get clarity is with a plus and minus balance sheet. It's sometimes called a Franklin Close.

Example: *Should I look for a new job?*

Plus	Minus
I'm bored with what I do	It's easy work

A new job will bring new challenges. There's no opportunity for growth at the current job	I will lose my comfortable security
I'm not fulfilling my potential	I like the people I work with
I will probably be able to get higher pay, because I have new skills and my present company hasn't given me a pay rise in two years	I manage on what I currently earn
I could work longer hours or further away if necessary. The children have left home	It's great living close to work. No traffic hassles.

Conclusion: ....

Your choice will depend on your values, priorities and Big Picture goals.

Lateral thinking to help in decision-making

It's useful to think outside the square about an issue. The father of lateral thinking is Edward de Bono. You may be interested in studying his work on Six Thinking Hats. It gives a very clear way of clarifying your thoughts on any issue. It's often used in the workplace when making important decisions.

In very simple terms, you mentally put on one coloured hat at a time and consider the question under review only from that perspective. Then move on to another colour. You don't pass to another style of thinking until you've gone as far as you can with the hat in use.

White Hat: Information. What are the facts?

Red Hat: Feelings. What do I feel about this?

Black Hat: Judgment. What is wrong with this?

Yellow Hat: Benefits. What are the good points?

Blue Hat: Thinking. What thinking is needed?

Green Hat: Creativity. What new ideas are possible?

As with planning, the process of focused consideration clears the brain and helps us see the real issues much more quickly than when we churn things round and round in our minds. Once we learn to make decisions quickly, trusting our choices, we save time.

Creative thinking is not a talent, it is a skill that can be learnt.

Edward de Bono

Does it really matter which decision I make?

Successful people make decisions quickly. They're not necessarily always right, but they do make them. 80 percent of all decisions should be made now! And many times it doesn't matter what the decision is, as long as one is made. Insistence on having all the facts first can dramatically slow up results. Use mistakes as a learning process. Accept risks as inevitable – within the parameters of common-sense, obviously.

Some personalities will find it harder to make quick decisions. They're what I call Owl personalities. (See Chapter 9 for more on personality types). They need all the data before they feel comfortable; they double-check every detail before they can recommend any course of action. They hate being wrong, or even *possibly* wrong. They make great accountants, lawyers, researchers and computer programmers. Try to avoid having them in company roles which need quick decision-making skills. If you're an Owl, learn to listen to your intuition (it's becoming widely recognised as a legitimate business tool.) Practise quick decision-making in small things, such as what meal to have at a restaurant. You might get to like it eventually!

If you don't have good fact-finding processes in your company, try and institute some. If you've got some good ideas, present them to your boss. Maybe ask for the subject to be put on a staff meeting agenda. If you're the boss, listen to what your staff are saying. Be open-minded. Most staff want the same objectives as their employers – an effective, smoothly functioning company.

One company I worked for required that every time a client asked the cost of one of our products, which was outside the normal price-range, we had to ask our boss for a price. It was very frustrating and Time-wasting, especially if he'd left for the day and wasn't taking calls. After I left the company they brought in specific guide-lines – a bit late for me!

PERFECTIONISM

Perfectionism is closely related to procrastination (which we'll talk about in much more depth in Chapter 12). If the bulk of a task is finished, it may not be necessary to complete to a very high degree of perfection. (Don't fall into the trap of never completing something, however. And it's *not* okay to leave work lying around. Put things away as you go!)

Joseph was a salesman for a meat processing export firm. He received a request via his manager that the CEO wanted the figures for live lamb exports to the Middle East. He wondered how much detail was required but decided that, since it was the Big Boss who wanted the information, he'd go the extra mile with presentation.

He beavered away for about four hours, putting together a lovely report with graphs, flow charts and colour.

A couple of days later he saw the CEO in the lunch-room. *'Thanks Joseph, for the figures. But – you didn't need to go to that much trouble. I just wanted the numbers.'*

Ask yourself and, if necessary, the boss, *'How perfect does this job need to be?'* The standard should be *'How much is necessary to achieve the desired results? How perfect does it really need to be?'*

If you've got a few perfectionist traits, try these thought-starters:

- Is it quicker to quickly add a hand-written file note or should it be typed?
- Can this report be stapled, instead of expensively bound?
- Will a quick email suffice or is a full report or well-crafted document necessary?
- Does this document go to the client or is it just for internal use?
- Do I need to record the conversation in great detail or are a few jotted notes sufficient?
- If I've given a good verbal briefing to someone, do I really need to follow up with a lengthy email basically saying the same things?

If you work in a field which requires a high degree of accuracy, you may have to re-train yourself not to fiddle around crossing every *t* and dotting every *i*. Every time you catch yourself getting really fussy about loose ends, think *'Is this necessary, or am I indulging myself?'* I'm an ex-librarian – I've fallen into this trap multiple times. In your heart you know when you're going down that particular rabbit hole!

I've mentioned it before, but let's repeat a powerful question: *'What's the best use of my time right now?'*

Another common trap is when you find yourself saying *'I'll just tidy up this low-level paperwork and then I'll start on that big task.'* I'm a big fan of having a tidy desk, but if this is a default behaviour to avoid starting on difficult or complex or less enjoyable high-value activities, beware. You might be majoring in minor things, focusing on perfectionism in things that don't matter, to the exclusion of those that do. Are you procrastinating or is the tidy-up essential?

Completing low-priority tasks leads to stress, because they are not moving you closer to accomplishing the things that are important to you.

Brian Tracy

Learn to delegate non-essentials

Perfectionists often struggle to delegate. For example, the parent who says *'I can't leave Johnny to clean up the kitchen after tea – he never does it properly and anyway, I can do it so much faster.'* It seems so obvious when we say it but I'm sure you know many parents, but especially mothers, who fall right into that particular trap. Johnny isn't stupid; his parents are! They'll be cleaning up after him in some form or other all their lives unless they teach him to be responsible. Some managers fall into the same trap.

KEY POINT No. 21: *The worst use of time is to be doing very well what need not be done at all.*

SCREEN TIME AND TELEVISION

It was people working in the television industry who told me, years ago, that there's a direct inverse relationship between the amount of TV a person watches (and these days we would include any devices providing entertainment) and the income they're capable of earning. In other words, those who spend a lot of time being entertained by external sources are not stimulating their creative brain and will not be capable of creating higher income.

If you're at all concerned about the impact of screen time (not just TV) on us and our families, I can't recommend too highly that you look into the work of Dr Aric Sigman. He's an internationally respected psychologist and the author of many scholarly articles and several books, including *Remotely Controlled – How Television is Damaging Our Lives.*

Watching television is now the industrialised world's main pastime, taking up more of our time than any other single activity except work and sleep. According to the Broadcasters' Audience Research

*Board (BARB) in January 2004, by the age of 75 the average Briton will have spent more than twelve years of 24-hour-days watching television. The average six-year-old will have already watched more than one full year of their lives. When other screen time is included, the figure is far higher. Children aged 11 to 15 now spend 55 percent of their waking lives – 53 hours a week, seven and a half hours a day – watching TV and computers, an increase of 40 percent in a decade. (*This research was published in 2004). *More than half of three-year-olds now have a TV set in their bedrooms.*

... in industrialised societies, the findings are set to re-cast the role of the television screen as the greatest unacknowledged public health issue of our time.

Aric Sigman. Visual voodoo: the biological impact of watching TV. *Biologist* Vol 54, 1, Feb 2007.

What screen time is doing to our children's brains

There's a huge amount of research to show that screen-time distorts and damages our children's brains. The following list is a precis of some of Dr Sigman's points:

- When children are growing, they need to develop sustained attention or concentration. Screen-time, even if it's used for education, cultivates the opposite – divided attention.
- 80 percent of brain-growth occurs between the ages of 0 – 3. That's when most of the brain's connections are formed.
- There is a highly significant dose-response association between screen time (ST) and risk of type 2 diabetes, cardiovascular disease (CVD) and all-cause mortality among adults.
- Increased TV viewing has been consistently shown to be linked to increased body mass index (BMI) in both children and adults. The association appears stronger in young children.
- Preschool children who watch more TV are fatter and less active.
- Video game playing was found to significantly increase food intake in adolescents immediately after playing *and was not compensated for during the rest of the day.*
- A randomised controlled clinical intervention trial divided four to seven-year-olds into two groups. One had its TV and computer

viewing reduced by half; the other did not. After three years there had been a significant reduction in the BMI of those who had halved their screen viewing and relatively little change in those who had not.

Some suggestions for management of screen time:
- My technique when my children were young was to restrict viewing to one hour per night per child. If it wasn't a show of choice the others had to be out of the lounge, the only room that had a TV. None of them grew up to be big TV watchers.
- Some families don't have a TV at all. They report that their families are close, healthy, creative and well-adjusted. In large part they attribute this to having no television.
- Have a no-screens night once a week.
- Use a programme guide to sort what programmes you want to watch, rather than just turning it on and channel surfing.
- Monitor and control the time your children spend on hand-held computer games/media. Dr Sigman's ideal discretionary screen time limits are:

0 – 3 years	None
3 – 7 years:	0.5 – 1 hour/day
7 – 12 years:	1 hour
12 – 15 years:	1.5 hours
16+ years:	2 hours

- Parents must take into consideration how much time their children spend doing homework on computers before coming to a decision on discretionary screen time for their child.
- Be aware of the role modelling influence your own viewing habits may have on your children, along with the potential influence of background or *passive* media.
- Schools need to adopt a position on the amount of time children spend in front of a screen in and out of school and communicate this to pupils and parents.

You might want to do a quick analysis. How many hours are consumed by screen time in your home? And if you've got children, what proportion of their time is spent in play, sport and other non-screen activities?

An unbalanced diet of television will make anyone passive, un-motivated, apathetic, and ineffective. The key question to ask is *'What benefit will this programme be to me?'* If you've chosen to have some recreational viewing time, that's perfectly fine. However, if you really should be doing something else, you're frittering away your precious life.

Remember – any activity which is not, in some way, moving you in the direction you wish to go is a Time-Wasting activity.

KEY POINT No. 22: *Learn to focus on your highest priority activities, including recreation, and you'll crowd out potential time-wasters.*

CHAPTER 8 HOW TO RUN EFFECTIVE MEETINGS

ARE THEY UNNECESSARY CHIT-CHAT OR AN IMPORTANT COMMUNICATION TOOL?

Meetings are a form of communication and an essential part of business life, but too many are, at least in part, a waste of time. Studies show some horrifying statistics. From a Harvard Business Review survey published in July/August 2017: *'We surveyed 182 senior managers in a range of industries. 65 percent said meetings keep them from completing their own work. 71 percent said meetings are unproductive and inefficient. 64 percent said meetings come at the expense of deep thinking. 62 percent said meetings miss opportunities to bring the team closer together.'*

- How many meetings do you attend every month?
- How many hours do they take out of your life?
- Are they productive hours, or do you spend most of the time wishing you weren't there?
- Has it ever occurred to you that probably most of the other participants also wish the meetings were more productive?
- Have you ever counted the combined dollar cost to the company of having a group of people in a poorly-run meeting?

OKAY PEOPLE... FIRST ITEM FOR DISCUSSION — "DO WE REALLY NEED THIS MEETING?"

WHY DO WE HAVE MEETINGS?

In *The Effective Executive,* management writer Peter Drucker says *'One either meets or one works – one cannot do both at the same time.'* While this is a very pessimistic view, it does highlight a common opinion.

Focusing on the following points may help you get better value from the time you have to spend in meetings:

- Do you really need it? Are there other ways you could achieve the same results, without taking everyone away from their work to sit round a table? Possibilities: a questionnaire, phone calls, a short memo, brief one-on-one conversations as you walk around, information on the company intranet.
- Only invite those who need to be there. Don't waste the time of people whose input won't be needed on that occasion, even if they normally attend.
- Beware of having a meeting because you don't want to take responsibility for a decision you should be able to make. Even if you haven't got all the facts, you'll usually be right and if you're not, it's a learning experience.
- Have a scheduled one-on-one weekly meeting with each member of staff. This gives both the staff member and the manager an opportunity to air their agendas. Managers – make sure you don't monopolise the time. Expect your staff to come with their questions and possible solutions and be prepared to give them your focused time. If they raise questions on other days, ask if they can wait until their meeting. (If the matter is critical, obviously you'll deal with it immediately).

This idea will only work if both parties are committed to keeping this weekly appointment and not letting anything except major emergencies interfere. The manager of a team of twenty became very disciplined about the one-on-one system and found that spontaneous interruptions between he and his staff were significantly reduced. Also, the weekly team meeting became much shorter and relevant to everybody present. The staff were happier; they got personal attention and didn't waste time sitting through each other's problems.

Some managers feel they're too busy for these regular one-on-one catch-ups. They tend to be the ones beavering away at their desks late, dealing with all the 'issues'. Some of said issues would have been headed off at the pass if they'd invested a little more time just talking to their people informally.

GUIDELINES FOR GROUP MEETINGS

AGENDA

1. Have an agenda, which everyone should be able to contribute to, circulated at least a few days before the meeting. The benefit of this is no hidden surprises, no sudden dumping of issues. When people are unprepared there's a much higher likelihood of misunderstandings and dissension.
2. The purpose of an agenda is to tell people what will be discussed, why and what you want to achieve. If they know this beforehand, they can come prepared. This will help reduce inefficient, unproductive meetings. Never assume, however, that people will come prepared. Tell them what you want them to bring and what contributions you want.
3. Don't allow written reports to be read out. Circulate them beforehand or with the minutes. Discuss only the vital items.
4. Place the most important items at the top of the agenda. Then, if someone has to leave early, the critical topics have been discussed. Without prioritising agenda items, it's very easy to spend half an hour at the start on something low-level and then be rushed at the end on the key topics.
5. Where possible, get closure on each item. No point in having another meeting if agreement can be reached now. At the very least, make sure there's some progress.
6. Be structured. Don't dodge all around the agenda. Think how a court of law runs. What would happen if they had some general discussion, some defence witnesses, some prosecution witnesses, more generalities, dodged back to an earlier witness, and so on? Confusion and mayhem! Stay focused on one issue at a time, finish and then move on.

To this point, watch the hilarious 1974 Video Arts training video *Meetings, bloody meetings* starring John Cleese. You'll find it online. If that doesn't shake up your perceptions, nothing will!

7. Give trivia the time it deserves. If something is urgent but relatively unimportant, put a time limit on discussion.

TIME

1. Have a clear definite start time and begin when you say. The organised people who arrive on time should not be made to suffer for the slackness of others. If someone comes late, don't stop and recap – it's the latecomer's responsibility to catch up after the meeting, or from the minutes. Their tardiness expresses their disregard for other people's time. If the chairperson is regularly late, start without them. Some managers won't allow late-comers into the room. The embarrassment about being shut out is often enough to fix bad habits. (I had it done to me once – I know!)

2. Set a finish time and stick to it. Inform attendees of it before they come. Then people can plan their next appointment with confidence. Vital items might sometimes take longer than expected but if they've been placed at the top of the agenda, it should be rare that they cause a time over-run. Meetings (and any work, if we let it) will expand to fit the time available.

3. If you set meetings prior to lunch or near end of day, it reduces the temptation to go over time.

4. Try to avoid long meetings in the morning. Most people are more productive then. If the first few hours are spent in meetings they may never catch up with their day's tasks.

5. Encourage people to leave straight after the meeting. It keeps the momentum of the day going.

6. Don't waste the time of the whole group on something which can be easily handled by a sub-committee of two or three. If ten people each speak for two minutes, twenty minutes have gone for ever!

7. How about a stand-up meeting – especially if there are only a few things to sort out? When we get comfortable we'll usually take longer. Some of my clients regularly have morning stand-up meetings and get through their agendas very quickly.

GENERAL POINTS

1. If you don't know the purpose of a meeting, find out. If the chairperson hasn't yet learnt to inform attendees in advance, you can be pro-active about it. Find out what you need to prepare. Be willing to contribute. If you go along with the mind-set of *not another boring meeting* you might as well not be there.

2. If meetings you attend are not well run, what are you doing about it? Bring it up as an agenda item. Again, be Proactive – don't just moan and assume that someone else will fix things.

3. Before the next meeting, review the minutes to be sure you've done what you said you would.

4. For much more in-depth information on running effective meetings, get a copy of my *Getting a Grip on Effective Meetings.*

KEY POINT No. 23: *Keep practising. A well-run meeting is a work of art.*

How to save hours per week in improved meetings

In Chapter 4 I promised you the specific techniques that Kate and her colleagues applied that produced enormous time-savings. They were in the marketing department of an international FMCG (fast moving consumer goods) company and for some months worked with me to improve their processes.

Kate's first week after her coaching:

1. Instead of driving into the city twice in that week she asked two of her agencies to come to her office. It might not have saved time for the agencies, but after all, whose money was it? **Saving: 3 hours of travel time.**

2. She was invited to a very important presentation, in her own building, for a major client. It was moderated by one of her colleagues. In the past Kate would have sat through the full event – over 5 hours. Instead she asked to be called when required for her contribution. That only took 45 minutes. **Saving: 4 & ½ hours.**

3. With her better meeting management skills (using some of the strategies outlined in this chapter), she kept an internal

---

meeting (that previously had always gone overtime) on track and to time. **Saving: at least ½ an hour.**

Total time saved that week: 8 hours. Add to that the other work she *did* achieve and you can see why Kate was excited about her output and progress the next time we talked!

Karlea, another project leader, also had regular external agency meetings. One of her frustrations was lack of clear outcomes and clear incisive next steps from some meetings. So, for the next one her major focus was to make sure 'next steps' were in place before they all left the room. The sharp intention resulted in far better results than previously.

She was also aware of not involving her colleagues unnecessarily. Instead of five people sitting through a 1 & ½ hour meeting (7 hours 30 minutes of company time), by inviting people only for the part relevant to themselves the total time invested became 2 hours 50 minutes, **a saving to the company of 4 hours 40 minutes.** To calculate the dollar saving to the firm, you'd need to also factor in things like cost of desk, phone, building, support staff and of course the opportunity cost of so many staff not getting on with other vital work.

CHAPTER 9 DELEGATION – HOW TO GAIN TIME THROUGH LEVERAGE

Delegation is one of the main keys to improved time management. It requires us to outline projects, assign responsibilities, set deadlines and check results. In other words, passing work on to others forces us to be organised. If the people around you clearly understand what you're asking, delegation will reap you great benefits. If we do it badly, it's not only a major time waster but also demoralising for the team.

In this chapter we'll look at nine key elements for effective delegation to help you share the load:
1. Understand the benefits.
2. Identify the barriers.
3. The keys to good delegation.
4. What you can delegate.
5. If you've got no-one to delegate to.
6. When you're the one being delegated to.
7. Upward delegation – watching out for other people's monkeys.
8. Sharing responsibility responsibly.
9. Personality types and how they relate to delegation.

THE BENEFITS OF DELEGATION
I'm sure Mark Twain believed in delegation. He said: *'To be good is noble, but to teach others how to be good is nobler... and much less trouble.'* He even had Tom Sawyer demonstrate the point, in his book of the same name. Tom had to whitewash Aunt Polly's picket fence but his friends wanted him to play. So he tricked them into believing that only the lucky ones would be allowed to partake in the wonderful sport of fence painting. Tom got to supervise while all his mates did the painting. What a master of delegation!

It's a learned skill and once you master it you'll dramatically increase your work output. It changes from what you can do to what you can oversee. Good delegators give their subordinates as much responsibility and authority as they're able to accept, while but at the same time maintaining control. Paradoxically, good delegators increase their own power by sharing it with others. It helps you build a cohesive team and allows your colleagues room to grow professionally. It also increases your people skills by forcing you to learn more about effective communication. But, just because we know that good communication is key, doesn't mean it's easy. A Harvard management specialist, after much research, concluded that the ability to communicate clear expectations was a manager's most important leadership and motivational tool.

Above all, effective delegation frees you to be more productive and creative.

KEY POINT No. 24: *Most manager don't have enough time to complete all their responsibilities. Delegation is the answer.*

A very large soil and garden supplies franchise in my region was developed by a man who left school at fifteen, unable to read. His first job was laying lawns for pensioners with a shovel, rake and barrow. Only when he was in his thirties did a specialist discover that he suffered from a condition called Irlen Syndrome – a perceptual processing disorder, not an optical problem. With tinted glasses and some coaching, the world of books opened up to him and he became an excellent reader.

His business increased before he could read, so he had to delegate the office tasks. As a result, delegation became one of his greatest strengths. He learned to rely on the skills of his staff – probably more than any business owner I've met – and his people responded well to the extra responsibility. It wasn't uncommon for his office staff to tell him: *'We've got everything in hand. Why don't you go for a drive in your truck and think of more ideas?'* The business grew exponentially.

He didn't abdicate – he empowered them. At all times he knew exactly what was happening but let his people do what they did best while he focused on the skill he'd been forced to learn – working *on* the business, not *in* it.

A really important thing to remember: we delegate *responsibility* but not *accountability*. At the end of the day, the buck stops with the manager, even if the employee got it wrong. Almost always, I believe it's the manager's fault if there's a mistake. At some point there's been a lack of supervision or training.

BARRIERS TO DELEGATING
In spite of the advantages, many people resist learning to delegate. They have a really good selection of 'reasons', most of which don't stand up too well to close inspection.

Are any of these familiar?
- If I want something done properly, I have to do it myself.
- I'm too busy to train staff. It's quicker to do it myself.
- I'm scared I'll lose control.
- I don't want to impose on my staff by asking them to do more work.
- I don't like asking, in case my staff don't like me.
- I'm afraid my subordinates will outshine me and one day be promoted above me.
- I can't trust my staff.
- I'm not very good at explaining how to do a task. It's easier to just get on and do it.
- I don't know how to delegate.
- There's no-one to delegate to. We're already short-staffed.
- We can't afford mistakes.
- Most of our decisions are made under crisis situations. I can't trust my staff to act on my behalf.

If you identify with any of these, help is here!

KEYS TO GOOD DELEGATION
Effective delegation rarely come naturally – many of us find it hard to step back and help others do the work we used to do.

There are various levels of delegation. Progressively, by a process of education, supervision, coaching and practise, true delegation (passing a complete task over) is achieved.

Before you delegate, ask yourself these questions:
- What exactly is the job? Do you understand it enough to explain it clearly? Until you can explain it clearly, you won't get good results.
- Have you got the right person for the job? Don't waste your resources trying to pick acorns off an apple tree. For example, don't expect an outgoing salesperson to do the typing for an extended period, or a quiet, backroom person to fill in long-term as a receptionist. They will probably neither do the job well nor enjoy it and you'll almost certainly end up frustrated and dissatisfied.

Once you've chosen a suitable person:
- Carefully describe the result you want.
- This next point is vital: have your chosen person explain back to you what they understand. This takes time initially, but often saves hours at the other end.

  One phrase **not** to use is *'Do you understand?'* It's a very useless closed question. No-one wants to look silly. Most of us, if asked that question, will say yes and then try and work it out later.

  Instead, have some open-ended questions ready. I learnt this with my first employee, a sweet young girl with not a lot of self-confidence. In order to relax her I found I had to take responsibility for the possibility that she hadn't understood. I'd say: *'I've probably forgotten something. What would you like me to go over again?'* This made it safe for her to ask for further directions.

  Or you might say something like: *'Tell me how you'll go about it'* or *'Where will you start?'* or *'How did you do this in your last job?'*
- While we're on the topic of questions, seek to use them at all stages. I believe that there is no greater delegation skill than that of asking quality questions. If we just *tell* we have no idea what our delegatee really knows.
- Tell your chosen person what authority or resources they have access to. If you've given them access to resources they wouldn't normally have, tell anyone else who may question them, or who needs to know.

KEY POINT No. 25: *The most powerful skill for effective delegation is asking great questions.*

- Be clear about when the task needs to be completed.
- If necessary, demonstrate. Then let them have a practise while you watch and guide. John Cleese, of *Fawlty Towers* fame, is credited with the phrase (probably in one of his *Video Arts* training videos) *'I do it normal, I do it slow, I do it with you, and off you go.'*
- Leave them alone to get on with the job. It can be very off-putting for a boss to watch, once you've had some instruction.

When John was a student he had the chance to work for two hay-making contractors during his university summer holidays. One man told him how to drive the big unwieldy tractor and bailer round the paddock and then stood supervising, yelling every time he went even fractionally crooked. He ended up feeling really jittery and incompetent.

The next day he had his second interview. The potential employer explained how to use the machinery, gave him a bit of practise while he quietly watched and then went away for about half-an-hour, saying, *'Have a go by yourself. I'll come back in a while and see how you're getting on.'*

No prizes for guessing which contractor he chose to keep working for. Once he'd had some 'mistake time', he quickly got the hang of the machinery and became very good at his job.

- Set a time to review and inspect what you've delegated. If the delegatee is inexperienced the review time might be as little as five minutes, but it is important to give them time on their own.
- Did you know that most of us can only hold between two to four instructions in our head at any one time? Don't explain too much at once.

- Delegators often forget how long it took *them* to learn the task they're now showing someone else. Be realistic. (After all, you don't want your new staff member to be too much quicker off the mark than you, do you!) You may have to show them more than once. That's okay. If you start to feel impatient, just remember the last time you got annoyed at a new piece of equipment or software.
- Remember always – once someone is trained, managers should direct what needs to be done, not how it's done. Otherwise we run the risk of being micro-managers.
- Empowered staff, given the opportunity to take responsibility, will almost always work to their maximum instead of working to rule. If they feel that they *own* their job they'll be much harder on their own time inefficiencies. On the other hand, an employee who doesn't feel very important won't worry about the little time-wasters that cuddle in for comfort.
- Praise and encourage. If more people recognised the magical power of praise they would use it constantly. Praise gives life, empowers people, builds self-esteem and confidence. It gives them confidence that they're doing a good job and are appreciated.
- All workers, at every level, want credit and recognition for work done well. Not only does it make them feel better, they are actually able to do more.

Many years ago I heard the story of a young girl working for a restaurant chain. A coach, helping her build self-esteem, encouraged her to embark on a programme of thanking and acknowledging her fellow workers. This included writing them notes and sending them little cards. She was fairly new in the company – certainly not one of the management.

About a year later, the company managers came to visit this particular outlet to find out why their results were consistently better than other outlets. Everything pointed to this young girl. By her positive, genuine appreciation of her colleagues she had lifted their morale. This outflowed to the customers who enjoyed their eating experience more, spent more and recommended the restaurant to others. The young woman was promoted to a management position and given a healthy pay rise.

Even one person can make a difference.

KEY POINT No. 26: *Praise releases energy, criticism kills it.*

WHAT CAN YOU DELEGATE?

Delegate anything that someone else can do – even if only 60 percent as well as you. By passing a task on, you're free to work on something other people can't do. If it takes 40 percent of your time to explain, review, supervise and in early stages, possibly finish the task, that still frees up 60 percent of the time you would have otherwise spent. And the other person will improve and quickly free up *more* of your time – if you teach them correctly.

One caution: When you delegate, be aware of the workload of others. Passing a task on may seem like efficiency to you, but if you overload your staff you may be creating mayhem for everyone, including yourself. Some staff will have enough confidence to let you know but if they don't, you might end up like the manager in the story below.

Susan was a senior manager in a logistics company. At a workshop she told the story of two staff members in her team.

Laura was quite assertive. If she felt Susan was overloading her, she was very quick to let her know.

Bill, on the other hand, seemed to be the ideal employee. Whatever Susan asked of him, he willingly said: *'No problem, I can handle that.'* He took all the work she gave him. She was most impressed. Many times she wished Laura was more like Bill, although she couldn't fault the work she turned out.

One day Bill was away sick. They needed a file he was working on, so Susan had to dig into his desk. To her horror she uncovered a drawer full of unfulfilled promises, of overdue work, of tasks procrastinated on.

IF YOU'VE GOT NO-ONE TO DELEGATE TO

In today's business environment, many companies say they haven't got enough people resources to delegate to. Sometimes that is so, but often, when they look more closely they find they're not using their people effectively. Staff are often under-utilised in one area and over-worked in another.

There are usually inefficiency loop-holes that can be plugged. Maybe there's a communication block somewhere up the line. Perhaps the owner or manager hasn't learnt to let go yet. Commitment is self-generating – it cannot be forced, but the fertile soil in which it grows is effective delegation.

Or perhaps you're self-employed or run a small business with a handful of staff. You might quite correctly say: *'I haven't got anyone else to delegate to, and I can't afford to take anyone on.'*

I know this story well – it was my story in the early days of my business. My observation is that, generally, we need someone before we can quite afford them. When we reach this point, we can't afford not to have help if we're serious about moving on and being successful. There's a fine line to walk here. It's essential to not over-extend yourself financially to the point of risking your business. However, beware of limiting yourself with small thinking.

Your key questions are:
- How much can I generate per hour if I'm working on my top-value activities?
- How much would I have to pay someone else to do the lower-value tasks I'm currently doing?
- Which parts of what I do can only I do?
- What can I train someone else to do?

While you're doing those low-value activities you're effectively paying yourself at the rate of a less-skilled person. You block yourself from higher dollar returns, simply because you can't do two things at once.

If you're not sure whether to hire someone else to help with your work, try this simple quick exercise:
- Draw three columns on a piece of paper. The first column takes

up most of the page.
- In the first column write down all the tasks you currently do in a week. Include tasks done less regularly, e.g. monthly.
- In the second column record the number of minutes or hours per week that you're currently spending on each task. For the less regular ones, just estimate how much time it might be if you were to break them into weekly activities. This exercise is just a rough guide; an approximate guess is all you need. ***Do not*** spend hours on a complex analysis. You should be able to do this in about an hour, spread over a few days.
- In the third column record the number of minutes or hours that someone at a lower pay rate would probably take on any of the tasks that could be shared – if you had another 'someone'.

When I first did this exercise, early in my self-employment life, I realised with shock that I was working eighty hours per week. No wonder I was starting to feel burnt out! However, the third column was the real shocker. I discovered that if I had some inexpensive help I could pass over nearly forty hours of low-level admin-type tasks.

Within six weeks I'd found a lovely young lass from a subsidised work scheme whom I job-shared with a friend in a similar overloaded situation. I had Lilian for only eighteen hours per week but that was enough to help me get my head above water and improve my processes and income.

A few more questions to help your thinking:
- What benefits can you see for yourself in having an assistant?
- What will you do with the time which is freed up?
- What impact will that have on your business and your life?
- What *really* stops you from hiring someone?

How to find the right person:
If you've tried the analysis above, the list you've just written is essentially a job description for the person you're about to look for. But if you've not hired someone before, finding the right person can be daunting. I like writing what I call a *'job description to God'*. Be as detailed and specific as possible about not only the tasks he or she will do but also the qualities you want. Anything you *don't* want, write

down from a positive perspective. For instance, instead of saying 'not slow' you'd write 'quick moving and fast on uptake' As I've already mentioned several times in this book, the magic power of focus is beyond understanding. By applying your mind on how to fix a problem instead of why you can't, you invoke a universal consciousness that draws the answer to you.

You don't have to believe me – just try it. What's the worst that can happen? If it doesn't work, no-one will know unless you tell them! And I promise that if you have clarity of mind, clear focus and a positive attitude, you will be amazed at what happens.

More tips on finding help:
- What about bringing in part-timers, or outside contractors for some of the tasks?
- Hire a student. Many universities and colleagues have hiring services. Do an online search in your country or region to find what's available.
- You'll easily find freelance contractors, many through your personal network. My web and IT guy Paul started contracting to me, and other small business owners, many years ago when he was about seventeen. His earnings funded him through uni. Every few years we meet for coffee but the work is done to fit his schedule, at his own home sixty miles away. He's truly awesome. I can throw him anything – he's so fast, smart and effective that I can't imagine using anyone else.
- Can some parts of your work be outsourced through online sources such as Upwork or Freelancer, using freelance providers from anywhere round the world? For example, the new cover for this book has been designed by Jeffrey in Singapore. These highly skilled and very cost-effective outworkers will work on short- or long-term projects.
- You may prefer to work through an intermediary company. Quite a number are now set up to act as the middle-man and find and manage offshore contractors for you.
- Who's under your nose? Family? Or family of staff? Children can learn life lessons disguised as business opportunities *and* we get help.

The entrepreneurial child

It was a sunny Sydney morning in May 1998. Kate and I were planning our next client newsletter. She was one of my two part-time assistants and the one who assisted with marketing activities. She turned to me and said: 'Robyn, you're wasting money with our newsletter.'

I looked at her in alarm. After all, everyone who knows anything about marketing knows that you need to keep in touch with your customers and prospects.

She chuckled at my response – clearly she'd been aiming at shock value! An explanation was needed. 'I don't mean we shouldn't do it. I'm talking about the work we do to get it out.'

At the time of this conversation we were sending out a two-page newsletter every couple of months to 600+ customers and good prospects in both Australia and New Zealand. One of Kate's duties was to take my content, format it, get the finished product photocopied down the road, print the address labels out of our database, stick labels on the envelope, fold and insert the newsletter in the addressed envelope and of course stamp it. In today's email world that sounds like a cumbersome task – and it was! If she had a better idea I was keen to hear it.

'My twelve-year-old son Dylan wondered if you'd consider out-sourcing some of the work. If so, he'd like to tender for the routine parts of the job.'

This sounded promising. She went on. 'I'll do the prep and printing of the newsletter as usual. Dylan would like to do the rest. If you're up for it, this is how we'll work out a rate. I'll use a stop-watch to see how quickly I can do the work he can do, we'll calculate a piece-rate cost based on my wage, and he'll then offer a piece-rate based on a significantly lower hourly rate. So, it won't matter how long he takes; the rate will be based on the number of items he processes. And I'll keep an eye on quality control, of course.'

Having raised six kids I've always been a huge believer in encouraging children's initiative and entrepreneurship. 'Go for it,' I *replied with enthusiasm.*

The next newsletter went out soon after. A few days later Kate arrived at work bearing Dylan's invoice. I looked at it with delight. It was a lot less than I would have paid his mother for the same work.

'This is great. What a clever boy. I really appreciate his initiative'.

'Oh, the story gets better,' *said Kate with a grin.*

'What could be better than this?'

'Dylan decided he could out-source too. He got a twelve-year-old friend to come and help do the stuffing and labels and persuaded his six-year-old brother to put on the stamps. The reward for his helpers was to take them to MacDonald's!'

WHEN YOU'RE BEING DELEGATED TO

If you're not happy with how you're delegated to, you may be partly at fault. Are you passive about poor delegation, unclear instructions, too much work at a time, or unclear deadlines?

Here are points to help:

1. If you understand what is required, repeat instructions in your own words. Don't be afraid to ask questions. I know a woman who writes out the instructions she's been given whilst taking a briefing and gets the delegator to sign.
2. If you don't feel you've got the skills needed to do a task, say so and ask for help – positively. Don't wimp out and say you can't do it. Make it clear that you'd like to learn but will need some help initially.
3. Establish how much authority you have for each project. Then you don't have to keep going back to the boss for approval of each step. Make sure anyone else who needs to know about your extra authority has been informed by your manager.
4. Where possible, when you have a problem to discuss with your boss have some solutions to suggest at the same time. You'll increase in confidence and your supervisor is very likely to be impressed, giving you a possible edge when promotions are being considered.

5. Ask when the job needs to be completed and how long you have for your part.

6. If the manager is one of the 'watch me while I do it' variety who doesn't understand about letting you practise, you'll have to be assertive and train them. Say nicely *'That's good. Now, please may I have a turn while you watch.'* Almost always they'll move to one side very willingly and say *'Oh, of course'.* Often they're showing you something they're very good at and just forget to give you a practise.

7. If your manager doesn't suggest a 'review and inspect' time, you need to ask for it. Say when you think you'll need a review and check when it's convenient for them. Also say that if you need help on any point you'll be asking. (All of this very politely and positively. No prizes for alienating the boss!)

8. Sometimes you may be unlucky enough to have an impatient and intolerant manager. If so, you may have to get quite assertive.

9. Ask how perfectly the job has to be done. If it doesn't need perfection, don't get bogged down, even if you have a sense of pride in superb workmanship. You're paid to produce results to the standard required.

10. If your boss is a procrastinator, develop your own action plan, put it in writing and tell him/her you'll be commencing by ... time unless you hear otherwise. Most procrastinators are delighted that someone is using their own initiative but be sensitive as to when and with whom this is appropriate.

11. If you have a manager who specialises in last-minuting, constantly loading yet another *very urgent* job on you, ask them to prioritise the work they give you. Have a list written up with the estimated amount of time each task will take. Say something like *'These are the projects I already have on hand. Please put them in order, so I know which to attend to first.'*

When they've done so, put the list in a very visible place and ask them to repeat the exercise each time they come in with more. You'll eventually train them! By this you achieve two things: the boss is happy because the most urgent things are attended to and you've put the responsibility of priorities on to them instead of becoming a martyr.

Too many willing workers suffer from anxiety caused by trying to meet unrealistic pressures and demands. They hate saying 'no', and over time will suffer because of it. Their health and personal life will suffer before they finally say 'enough' and then a surprised boss says, *'You should have told me how you were feeling'*. Human nature being what it is, many managerial types just keep on flogging the weary horse until it turns around and nips!

12. If you receive work from more than one person and there's contention between the authors of your work, let them slug it out between themselves. Say, very graciously (and you can't afford to have favourites in this one), *'If the two of you could please prioritise this list of work, I would really appreciate it. Then I know I'm doing the best I can for both of you.'*

13. As a last resort (and I'm not advocating mutiny!) don't be afraid to say 'no'. Follow it very politely with *'I'm sorry, but I just can't manage to fit that task in, unless I drop something off. What would you like me to leave undone?'*

UPWARD DELEGATION – WATCH OUT FOR OTHER PEOPLE'S MONKEYS!

This occurs when your subordinates have you working for them. If they keep asking for help when they could work out the answers, look out – that's a danger signal. When they ask you to finish something for them because you know more about it than them or ask you to do errands as you go past, look out – that's taking up your head space on their work, not yours.

Some years ago I experienced a classic example of this. At the time I was President of a business women's organisation, with the overall responsibility of making sure everything was ready for the monthly meeting. I had a great committee and usually everything flowed very smoothly.

The day before one of the meetings I had a call from the woman whose job it was to organise the raffle. She was a very effective real estate salesperson but always in a tearing hurry, whipping up a whirlwind of activity wherever she went. The conversation went something like this. *'Oh, Robyn, I haven't had time to organise the raffle this month. I've been so busy. Could you please do it for me?'*

I hesitated.

I could have done it, even though I was busy, and yes, it was my job to help my committee if they needed it. I almost said yes, but something made me strong. After all, there were still 24 hours to go and it should have dealt with long before this. And when was she *not* busy? It was a clear case of not enough forethought. I felt rather put-upon. At the same time it flashed through my mind that if we didn't have a raffle that month it wasn't the end of the world.

To my own surprise, being a naturally helpful sort of soul, I heard myself saying, *'No, sorry .... I'm busy too. I'll have to get you to handle it.'*

'Oh, okay,' was the resigned response.

The next night she was brightly selling raffle tickets. *'Glad to see you could manage the raffle,'* I said.

'Oh, it was no trouble really,' she said, laughing into my face. *'But I nearly got you, didn't I!'*

A lot of managers wrestle with the upward delegation issue. They say, *'I have to keep an open door – that's what I'm here for.'* They think they're doing their job when they have thirty interruptions per hour and then wonder why they go home frayed. They feel it would be de-motivating to shut the door and then hide in a different office to get away from their staff! What they're really doing is allowing their staff to be mentally lazy by not taking responsibility for their own actions. Of course it's easier to go and ask the boss! Silly boss. If you keep spoon-feeding them, you'll stunt their development and find yourself doing their work.

If you recognise yourself in this situation, try one of these ideas, or some variation:
- When you're confident that the staffer has the competency to do the work, ask them to come with two solutions to any problem they ask for help on.

- For someone less experienced, don't supply the answer immediately. Ask what their ideas are and discuss options and consequences. You want to know what they're thinking, what they know and what else you need to teach them.
- I strongly recommend you get hold of *The One Minute Manager Meets the Monkey* by Kenneth Blanchard, William Oncken, Jr, and Hal Burrows. I love this little book! You'll have the essence of it in half-an-hour. Once you've met the hard-pressed manager sitting at his desk on a Saturday, doing the work of his staff while they have fun on the golf-course, you'll think very carefully before you let your staff's monkeys (alias problems) hop on your back.
- Be less available to your team. You'll still be a responsible manager if you shut your door for an hour or so every day. You'll achieve more and they'll be encouraged to seek their own solutions instead of bothering you unnecessarily.

The benefits of making people think about the solutions before they come to you with the problems are:
- The other person becomes more confident with their own judgement (because they are almost always right when they take the time to think things through).
- You achieve more with less stress.
- The company becomes more effective.

SHARING RESPONSIBIILTY RESPONSIBLY
- Identify exactly what you want to delegate. Find an area in each project that can be given away. There's almost always some part that can be farmed out, even if it's only small.
- Be prepared to delegate challenging jobs as well as boring ones. When you give someone else the chance to learn your job, it frees you to move on to better things. If you help someone in your team to upskill, you create the opportunity for further advancement for yourself. Remember that like attracts like – if you show generosity you will attract it.
- Allow others the opportunity to shine and don't hog the credit. This builds team spirit and develops the self-esteem of the colleague concerned. If people are recognised for their contributions they

enjoy greater work satisfaction.

- Not everyone feels confident about handling more work. Sometimes you have to actively encourage people to take more responsibility. At one time I had to pass on a monthly task that I'd previously done to a very capable woman. For the next few months she kept asking me to check her activity. Eventually I realised I had to tactfully refuse, whilst reassuring her that she always did an excellent job. It was an ego trip at first to be asked but became a time-waster for both of us; nor was it helpful in building her self-confidence.

- People who won't take responsibility are either lazy or need gentle encouragement. Sometimes the best solution is just to drop them in at the deep end and make them answerable for their actions. (But only do that when you're quite sure they've been trained properly and can do the work.)

- If you are going to give a bigger than usual task to an employee, prepare them well in advance so they don't feel overwhelmed.

- Give colleagues an overall picture of what's required. Confusion due to inadequate communication is one of the major reasons for ineffective work from subordinates. All of us operate better when we have clarity of purpose. Show people how their efforts will contribute to the overall result.

- Allow 'cushions of time' so that if something goes wrong you still have time to correct. If checkpoints are established before commencement and the employee knows about them, the checking becomes a learning process for them, not a negative correction.

- Evaluate the risk of delegating. Ask yourself, *'What's the worst possible thing that can happen if I pass this job on?'* If the consequences are severe, either don't delegate or establish very regular checkpoints.

I've already mentioned *The One Minute Manager Meets the Monkey*. You might like to check Blanchard's other books as well. They give some very good techniques for training staff. Take into account the personality styles and experience of each person.

And if you'd like more in-depth help on being an outstanding leader, effective running of teams, how to give praise and feedback, practical communication strategies and much more, grab *Getting a Grip on*

Leadership which I co-wrote with American leadership specialist LaVonn Steiner.

Getting a Grip on Leadership

Required reading for everyone ... clear, practical, and easy to read ... gives readers guidance on actual implementation... Section on strategic planning with tracking tools the best I've seen.

Linda Knodel, Snr VP/Chief Nursing Officer, St. Alexius Medical Center, Bismarck, North Dakota, USA

PERSONALITY TYPES AND HOW THEY RELATE TO DELEGATION

Nearly everyone wants to understand more about the personalities of themselves and those closest to them. The more we understand the characteristics of others, the more likely we are to get the results we want from those at work and the more harmonious our home environment will be. Understanding takes the heat out of potential conflict; the end result is that our time is used more effectively. Instead of spending hours per week trying to mediate, sort out conflict and run damage control, we can get on with useful and productive activity.

Since the 4th century BC, philosophers have been trying to understand what drives us. Hippocrates, Plato and Aristotle all had their pet theories. In A.D. 160 the Greek philosopher Galen wrote about four basic personality types and in more modern times a big range of analysis tools have been developed. Most are excellent; it really depends who you first learn from as to which one you prefer.

My first introduction was via a very easy-to-understand book called *What Makes People Tick* by Des Hunt. In it he used the bird names of Eagle, Peacock, Dove and Owl to describe the various personalities. It sorts us into the most dominant of the following traits: warm and confident; warm and shy; cool and confident; and cool and shy.

Eagle

These little charmers are cool confident types. They have strong dominant personalities and usually naturally move into leadership positions. Their strength is that they work well without supervision. They don't need a lot of encouragement to perform and are highly motivated by results.

One of their major weaknesses is that they're not very good listeners. They also hate having their time wasted. They tend to snap under stress and then can't understand why others get upset. Some would call them bossy; they call it showing leadership.

If you want to get a favourable response from an Eagle have your facts straight, get straight to the point, be direct and for goodness' sake, don't nag! Give them just enough information to make a fast decision, without the superfluous detail, or they'll tend to snap your head off!

Peacock

Someone on your staff likes being centre-stage? They enjoy fun, parties, noise and quickly get bored if there's no-one else around? They'll almost certainly have a dominant Peacock style – the warm, confident ones of this world. Many salespeople, trainers, motivators and entertainers fit in here. They are great people people, and others (mostly) enjoy being around them. If you've got a job requiring people skills, look for a Peacock.

They're great starters, not such good finishers. Too much detail bores them. (How many sales managers tear their hair out because their salespeople are very sloppy and slow about filling in their paperwork?) Quieter souls think they are much too loud and pushy; they think the quiet ones are boring!

To get the best out of a Peacock, encourage and praise them. They thrive on it. They're energised by being around others and stressed by being on their own for too long. Don't put them in a lonely work environment – they won't be able to perform effectively. They need to know that they are appreciated and even when, in their heart of hearts they know they've done a good job, they still like to be told.

Dove

If we didn't have the peace-loving, supportive Doves, life would be pretty uncomfortable. These folk are the salt of the earth. They're warm and shy and enjoy being support people. They like being around other people as long as they don't have to take centre stage. If you want someone to do something, chances are it's almost always a Dove who offers. They make great listeners and sympathisers. Many nurses, counsellors and support people are Doves – they're happiest when people need them. If the people around them are unhappy, they're unhappy too.

Don't expect Doves to initiate, though. That's way outside their comfort zone. They prefer not to speak out in public meetings. It's very easy to crush a Dove and not even realise you've done so, for they find it very uncomfortable to stick up for themselves. Managers have to be more thoughtful with their Doves than their other more vocal staff.

Doves are the kind-hearted souls who'll sacrifice their own needs for the last-minuting Peacock, or the domineering Eagle who comes rushing in demanding something without checking what else the Dove has to do. These are the ones who have the hardest job to say 'no' to unreasonable demands.

Owl

You always knew owls were wise birds, didn't you! So are human Owls. Here we have the cool shy folk. They make great accountants, lawyers, researchers, programmers, scientists or any career that needs high accuracy in their work. They thrive on being right. In fact, the possibility of having to pass work in without time to check it several times is just about enough to bring on an anxiety attack. Their strength is their attention to detail.

Their weakness is that they find it very hard to make a quick decision. What if it was wrong!

The best way to get good results from Owls is to give them a good briefing and enough time to double-check their work before they have to deliver it. Don't expect them to be happy about a rushed job. Also, most of them won't enjoy a noisy environment with lots of interaction. They prefer a 'smattering of shush', so they can get on and do their job well.

We're all mixtures of these types and most of us have two dominant styles. Only occasionally do we find someone who is so dominant in one category that the other styles hardly get a look-in. (We discover our style by filling in an 80-question sheet which is accessed through licensed agents.)

I've observed that most companies have a predominance of Doves and Owls, which is probably just as well. You know the old saying 'too many Chiefs and not enough Indians', don't you? And fancy having a whole company of Peacocks. There'd never be any work done – they'd all be too busy having a good time!

In terms of delegation, when deciding who to use for a task, think carefully about their personality styles. To get the best co-operation out of your workmates, work out how they like to be asked, under what conditions you'll get their best efforts and what support they need from you.

Give an Owl plenty of time and detail, give a Peacock plenty of praise and interaction with others, appreciate your Doves and don't take them for granted and *never* waste the time of an Eagle.

What great tips are you starting to apply?

You'll be amazed at the impact when you put into practise even a few things ... **for *small hinges swing big doors.***

If you've not yet got them, remember your **free** audio downloads wait for you at http://gettingagrip.com/digitalgifts

When you register to get your downloads you'll also receive a well-spaced supply of ongoing time tips and practical help. Should you wish to unsubscribe at any time, it's as easy as one click. We don't spam you and *never* share your details.

CHAPTER 10 SURVIVING THE NEVER-ENDING TORRENT OF EMAIL

Love it or hate it – email is part of our lives. Hardly anyone wants to go back to the (comparative) snail-speed delivery of information of pre-email days. But – almost all of us moan about the volume, the sense of urgency and the frequent overload generated by email.

A cluttered Inbox is a stressor. It's impossible to ever clear it for more than a few minutes, yet a desire for completion subliminally affects most of us. So, we live with constant and insidious pressure, knowing that more and more 'stuff' is yelling through the thin walls of our computers, phones or other devices – just waiting to trip us up the minute we take a peek. And I don't know many who haven't felt the irritation of ploughing through a ridiculous amount of emails after a holiday.

Let's look at this issue of pressure caused by incompletions. There are two questions to consider:
- Is it reality or just perception?
- Are there things we can do to reduce that load?

Part of the answer is mind-set. The other is strategies.

MINDSET FIRST
You knew I'd say that, didn't you! See email as useful but don't allow it to dominate or be the sole driver of your priorities.

If you've already started to implement my earlier recommendations about focusing on the Big Picture you'll not be surprised to hear me suggest that most email fits into the Reactive/Responsive category. The top-line solution is to take charge of when and how frequently you respond (rather than react) to it.

The medium *is not* the message – don't let it boss you around. Email is only a method of data delivery. Let's not become myopic about keeping the numbers down when really all we need to focus on are the truly useful messages. How much of what you receive every day is of *real* value? Of the rest of it, how much could be received in another form, reduced, re-routed or eliminated?

Note: There are always multiple ways to do techie things. I've kept this short list of strategies deliberately simple. I've also not bothered with clever apps – there's always something new coming on the market.

STRATEGIES
The first two tips of this list have been mentioned in Chapter 7 and I promised I'd expand on them. To many people, at first glance they seem counter-intuitive.
1. Turn off the alerts on your computer and phone.
2. Don't do email first thing in the day.
3. Use Rules – they're magical.
4. Chunk your response times – don't automatically deal with email as soon as it arrives.
5. Is email really the best medium?
6. Signatures save time – they're actually templates.
7. Save typing by using the Click and Drag function.

TURN OFF THE ALERTS
I've already discussed the severe penalty we pay if interruptions dominate our day. It's incredibly difficult to achieve anything solid when our attention is constantly disrupted.

Computers. If you're an Outlook user the pathway is File, Options, Mail, Message Arrival and untick all four notification options. On a Mac choose the Apple menu, System Preferences, then click Notifications, Mail and choose None.

If you work in a role that really does require you to respond rapidly to certain requests or people, I'll tell you shortly how to manage that for email.

Phones. Go through Settings and turn off all or most of your notifications. You'll have your own 'must-know' priorities but think very carefully about what you *really* need to be interrupted for. For example, the only notification I always keep on is texts. When I'm travelling overseas and friends are likely to contact me I'll also activate the WhatsApp alert. If I'm working with an Upwork contractor I'll turn on that notification for the duration of the project. But email – absolutely always off. Facebook, Twitter and LinkedIn the same. I do *not* want to know that someone's just posted about their lunch or holiday or that some influential idiot in another country has yet again done something stupid.

DON'T DO EMAIL FIRST THING IN THE DAY

This often draws a gasp of shock and sometimes outrage from listeners or readers. I've even had hate mail!

Why? Many people have been brain-washed into thinking they have to look at it to set their day's priorities. Really? If you've got this far in the book you'll know my answer to that (normally) faulty idea! Or they think, *'I'll just take a quick check before I start my work'* and before they know it, an hour or two of their precious day has disappeared. They've just been sucked into other people's priorities instead of their own. Problem is, for many of us the medium is more than seductive – it's addictive.

If your work is very responsive, it might be the second thing of the day, *after* reviewing your day's priorities. (Or third, if coffee is required before the brain engages!). However, for many people it could be mid-morning or even later. It depends on your role and the day's work.

Some possible exceptions:
- If you work across time zones and need to review last night's mail before you can start work.
- If you're in a customer-focused role that requires rapid response.
- You're the front-line PA/administrator or support person for rapid response colleagues or senior management and part of your role is to keep an eye on their email.
- You'll be away from your computer for the rest of the day. A quick morning check gives peace of mind.

Variations:
- One of my legal clients, who often receives instructions overnight

from offshore clients, checks his mail on his iPhone while he waits to give his teenage son a ride to school. He then has peace of mind and can get straight to his already-planned priorities when he hits the desk.

- Many people check mail on their phones whilst riding public transport to work. Most of us won't be tempted to get into a long response session on those small screens and keyboards. Mind at rest, we can then ignore email until the appropriate time of the day. One caution: If you do this on your phone, turn anything that needs further attention later in the day back to Unread so you don't lose sight of it.
- Every now and then have a non-email day. It won't die from neglect. Yes, you have to catch up the next day, but you'll have given your brain a chance to de-tox. Very good for the health! An increasing number of companies are instituting occasional 'Email-Free Days'. I've also heard of regular 'Email-Free Fridays'. Doesn't it sound like wonderful freedom!
- On a daily basis only deal with the top-level priority mails and leave the rest for a catch-up session, say once a week. This is what I do. It's another example of chunking tasks. Then I plough through the assembled 'might be useful' plethora of unread 'stuff' for a couple of hours.

RULES – MAGICAL TIME-SAVERS
Very few people know how to use Rules yet they make a huge difference to your efficiency. When correctly set up, they save you filing time, make it far easier to keep your Inbox under control and simplify searches. (Since the majority of businesses use Outlook I'll give examples from that. Even if you use a different email programme this will give you an idea of what can be done.)

Many people know vaguely that Rules are useful. Some know that they can be created to assist in automatic filing of much of our mail. But even those who do know, often don't follow through – for fear that they'll lose sight of new mail. (I was in that category myself in the early years of email.) In fact, you won't lose anything – as long as you change one tiny action when you first go to your Inbox. I'll explain that shortly.

If you've taken my advice and turned off that distracting alert, I'll shortly explain how to set up the few notifications you *really* need.

What's the reason for filing mail into folders?
Even though most email programmes now have really good search functions, they're not always 100% reliable. Sometimes the indexing system has a stop-work meeting or stages a go-slow. Or, for no obvious reason, something really important eludes you. When that happens it's both tedious and annoying to try and remember key words, dates, names or subject lines. If you use folders for your important communications you'll have more peace of mind.

Plus, if you've been in the habit of filing mail after it arrives you'll save heaps of time with Rules. Manual filing becomes a thing of the past, at least for your regular correspondents.

In the logistics department of a national grocery chain, one of the staff receives an automated mail when a certain action happens – multiple times a day. He only needs to look at those mails on a Friday when he's preparing a report and checking for exceptions. He'd been clicking and dragging all of them into a dedicated folder multiple times a day, mainly to stop his Inbox being ridiculously overloaded. I showed him how to set up a Rule to direct them straight into the folder and also how to turn them from Unread to Read. He didn't need to know they'd arrived; only where to find them when he was ready. Delight is too small a word for his face when he saw the clutter vanish!

How to create a Simple Rule
Right-click on an email in your Inbox that you'd like to file automatically. A menu will open up. Choose *Create Rule*. (There are other ways to create them but this is my favourite.) In the dialogue box that opens you'll see the email address of the sender in the top box. If you want to save all correspondence from that person to only one folder, tick the top box. (How to manage a person who covers multiple topics is explained below.)

If you want all mail with a consistent subject line diverted to a dedicated folder, in *Subject contains* delete any words unique to that individual mail before you tick that box. If the subject line varies, ignore that line.

Then tick *Move the item to folder* and *Select Folder*. This will open up your entire list of folders, if you've got some. Highlight your chosen folder and click OK.

Selective notifications

Let's assume you've taken my strong recommendation and turned off all your notifiers. But you've got a boss or a difficult client who requires instant action as soon as their comms bounce into your Inbox. Tick the box *Play a selected sound* and then *Browse* to choose a .wav file (sound). This will override the global instruction to turn off all notifications.

How to set up folders whilst working in Rules

If you don't yet have folders for different topics, don't worry. You can create them as you go. Essentially, you're setting up a filing cabinet, only this one is electronic. In the Setup wizard, when you *Select Folder,* there's an option for *New.* One tip – when creating a new folder check carefully where it will sit. It will go to below whatever folder was highlighted in the dialogue box unless you choose differently.

The cool and sophisticated part!

Advanced Options covers all the variables, including adding a sound to the incoming mail of a specific person. Take a tour through all the screens and prepare to be delighted with all the additions, actions, inclusions and exceptions you can personalise.

For instance, suppose you want everything from your PR company with the word *Press Release* in the subject line to go to a Press Releases folder. In the first page of the *Advanced Options* Wizard you'd tick the *From* box and *with specific words in the message header*. In the Edit box below, click *specific words* (this will show up once you've ticked as directed in the top panel). Now you can add Press Release and any other words you need.

You'll almost certainly have a few people who send mail on multiple topics. Suppose you want most of the mail from Bill, your Administration Manager, in one folder but travel bookings he organises for you in a separate Travel folder. (And ask him to put the word *Travel* or *Bookings* in his subject line.) The description will then look something like this:

Apply this rule after the message arrives
from **Bill**
move it to the **Office** folder
except if the subject contains **Travel** or **Bookings**

To get all the travel mails into a Travel folder, set another *Simple* rule dealing just with that topic.

How can I keep track of new mail if it's automatically filed?
Here's the tiny behaviour change which solves the problem of possibly missing new items.

Instead of going to Inbox when you check new mail, go first to *Unread Mail*. Then it doesn't matter in which folder your mail has automatically filed itself. Everything unread shows up in this folder, patiently waiting your attention.

If you've not activated it you'll find it (shown in italics) under *Search Folders*, usually near the bottom of your entire list of mail folders. The first time you click on *Unread Mail* it will populate with any unread mail, no matter where it's sitting in your email system. (What you see *in Unread Mail* is a replica – the mail doesn't move.) Now click and drag the *Unread Mail* folder up to the top left *Favorites* panel for quick access. I have it immediately below *Inbox*.

How to keep track of future actions
Once you've opened a mail, if you go out of the *Unread Mail* folder, naturally the mail will disappear. If you haven't finished with it you have several simple options. The first two are my personal favourites.
- A right click will give you the choice to *Mark as Unread*. Very useful if you like to use the *Unread* folder as a form of To Do list. Some experts suggest creating an *Action* folder for these mails – I find that too easy to ignore but you might be less visually wired.
- If it's an appointment or big task you need to block time out for,

click and drag the email into an appointment in your Calendar. It will also stay in whichever email folder it was already filed in.
- If you use the Task function in Outlook (which not many people do – it's too hard to prioritise easily) you can also click and drag the entire email into Tasks.

If you receive mail on your mobile

A couple of cautions about Rules if you read your mail on a smartphone – there are some limitations. I find on my iPhone that the mail that has auto-filed into folders doesn't show when you go to the Mail icon on the home screen of your phone. If you're expecting something and don't see it, hit the *Back* button on the top left of the mail screen. (Choose the relevant Account at the lower part of the screen if you've got more than one account.) You're looking for your entire hierarchy of folders, with bold numbers beside the folders with new unopened content.

When you read mail on your phone the quickest way not to lose sight of a future action is to turn the read mail back to *Unread*. You can then be sure to see it when you reach your computer.

DON'T AUTOMATICALLY DEAL WITH EMAIL AS SOON AS IT ARRIVES

Here are some options:
- Set yourself regular checking times, but not in your prime creative time.
- Some people may need to check every 30 – 60 minutes. Others can chunk their activity to two or three times a day.
- Treat looking at your mail as a light break between more important tasks.
- Set a time limit and then turn the mail programme off when time's up.
- If you've got a big task that needs concentration, don't go near your emails until you've had a solid burst of time on the big job.

IS EMAIL REALLY THE BEST MEDIUM?

How often have you become tangled up in a long email ping-pong match, trying to sort out something that would be far better dealt with by a quick phone call? You might like the following strategy, implemented by one of my large clients with offices in several countries. They called it *Reduce Email Week*.

There were two parts to the strategy.

1. Everyone received a small laminated card to place in a prominent place on their desk or beside their computers. Here's what it said:

Reduce Email Week

Before you send an email ask yourself ....

- Do I need to send this?
- Can I deliver the message in person?
- Can I discuss this over the phone?
- Am I sending this email for the right reason?
- If I must send this have I copied in unnecessary people?

Remember – email is not a tool for communication, only information.

---

2. When each person logged on to the system every day that week a notice popped up saying, *'Remember it's REM week'*.

Results? Instead of firing emails all over the place, sometimes multiple times a day (including to people in the next room or cubicle) they all found themselves getting up and walking down the corridor, picking up the phone, or simplifying in other ways. **Everyone** commented on how much more they achieved and the self-monitoring questions became part of their company's email protocol.

SIGNATURES SAVE TIME

Your email (or digital) signature is a great shortcut. It's not just for real signatures, but anything at all that you regularly type. It's really a template or little macro, but inside your email programme. One click will insert the words or phrases you've saved (of any length) anywhere in the body of an email with just one click.

In Outlook this neat feature is accessed through Tools/Options/Mail Format/Signatures and then just follow the wizard. In Apple the pathway is Mail/Preferences/Signatures. (If you use any other email programme, check out your programme's Help menu.)

You can have as many signatures as you like, with the choice dependant on whom you're writing to. I have about twelve. For example:
- driving instructions to my office.
- workbook specifications for the printer.
- thanks for your enquiry.
- a short signature for regular or repeat correspondents.
- a comprehensive signature for formal or first time correspondents.

One little trick – set the default to *None* so you can choose the right words for that mail. Another Outlook peculiarity – you can't insert more than one signature. If you want your real signature in every template you'll have to copy and paste it in.

With your 'real' signature, don't forget to add your email address, postal, phone (and URL if you've got a website). It's like having a return address on the back of all mail leaving your company – saves time at both ends and addresses all needs. And don't forget, when you add your phone number and address, that possibly some of your mails will end up overseas. Put the country code, area code, and full postal address, including country.

CLICK AND DRAG
Let's suppose you've received an email that relates to a meeting you've scheduled or it requires you to set up a meeting. Or perhaps it's a big enough task to justify blocking out some dedicated time. What most people do is set up an appointment in Calendar, then retype the information or cut and paste using the shortcuts Ctrl + C (Copy) and Ctrl + V (Paste).

Instead, click on the email and just drag it to *Calendar*. Now all you have to do is set the appointment times. The entire email is in the body of the calendar item. And – the original email still sits patiently in whichever folder you dragged it from.

With that little trick under your belt, try doing the same thing with a new contact you want to transfer into your Contacts list. The smart little click and drag trick works there too. The only extra thing required, if you don't need to keep the content of the email attached to the new Contact's name, is to delete the email from the Notes section.

If you use the Tasks feature, it also works there.

KEY POINT No. 27: *Email is designed to serve us, not the other way around.*

CHAPTER 11 HOW TO MANAGE THE TREES LITTERING YOUR DESK!

When I speak at conferences or run workshops on this topic, the following phrase has people begging for a repeat as they grab pen and paper. I never know if it's for themselves or to whack some suffering friend, family or colleague with.

KEY POINT No. 28: *Every piece of paper, information or equipment is a symptom of a decision not made or an action not completed.*

It is true, isn't it. So, let's drill down and find out how we can make better decisions and complete our paperwork actions. Keeping track of where things *might* be takes lots of mental energy; trying to ignore mess takes even more. Do you remember, in the beginning of the book, I suggested that it's not time we're learning to manage so much as energy? On that basis, it's easy to see that anything that sucks our energy needs to be sorted out – and that includes our offices. You will feel so much better once you've applied the simple steps in this chapter.

Sorting out our messy environments is the fastest stress reducer in town. If you struggle in this department, hold your hat – relief is at hand and it's simple, once you know how.

MESSY OFFICES – WHAT STORIES DO THEY TELL?

I'm going to be very assumptive and presume that at least some of my readers are in a state of chaos; that their office or desk would give a graffiti tagger ideas. Those of you already perfect in this area – don't read on. Just pass this section to your struggling buddies. And if you're in a company that has already invested in technology to convert most of your business to the Cloud, well done. If you're in such a firm, you also probably don't need to read this. However, there are still a huge number of paper-burdened homes and businesses.

Because I enjoy cleaning out cupboards and creating workable systems (yes, I know that's weird!), I thought everyone knew how to do the steps you're about to read. I finally realised, when I started working in the field of productivity, that I was very wrong. The very idea of initiating a sort-out is enough to send some poor folks into a tail-spin, mainly because they don't know how to start. The whole task seems just too overwhelming!

The good news is that everyone I've worked with to conquer their chaos has been able to sustain order once they've got a good system in place. Some of the biggest strugglers with the worst mess have even gone on to help other people. The key is in breaking the task into small, simple steps and, if necessary, getting a friend to help you.

HOW BAD IS THE PROBLEM?

How much time do you (or your staff?) spend weekly in searching for mislaid information – both digital and in paper form?

'I know exactly where everything is!' is the common response when anyone comments on a clutterbug's littered desk. You know the one – it could be mistaken for the town tip.

Yes, you might approximately know where things are — but how much time do you spend rifling through to find the urgent report needed for the meeting in ten minutes? Or the expenses claim form that Accounts have been demanding for the last week? Where is the contact information for the new supplier? And the Marketing department reckon they sent the proof of the new brochure that needs approval but you just can't lay your hands on it for the moment.

Sound at all familiar? What is *your* environment like?

If someone who doesn't know you walked into your office right now, what sort of person would they think you are? Messy people are less likely to be considered for promotion and less likely to be given new opportunities. Why? Because they're perceived as not managing their current load very well.

Or perhaps you've inherited someone else's office, left their junk in the cupboards and drawers in case it was important, never looked at it again and a year later wondered why you haven't got much space?

A cluttered environment indicates a cluttered mind. How did the mess happen? For many it's a case of worrying that if they put things away they'll forget them. From hard experience they *know* that putting things away equals losing sight of them. But think about what happens when we leave important things on the desk. Where does the next important thing go? Yep – on top! So that clever idea doesn't really work either, does it!

Let's try an experiment. When you next front up to your desk, take everything off it, pile the 'stuff' either on the chair or the floor, wipe the desk down, and then put back only the essentials. Notice how you feel when it's all clean and tidy.

Okay, that's a taste of freedom — now, what's to be done with the debris?

WELL, THOSE ARE THE ESSENTIALS —
NOW, WHAT DO WE DO WITH THE REST?

THE FOUR STEPS TO AN EFFICIENT WORKSPACE
1. Layout and equipment.
2. Clearing out the clutter.
3. Setting up good systems.
4. Maintaining the systems so you don't fall back into chaos.

LAYOUT AND EQUIPMENT

Obvious as the need for equipment and storage seems, I've seen many people try their hardest to be organised but with nowhere to put things.

If you're serious about a smoothly functioning workspace you need the right equipment. For anyone with paperwork to handle, it's impossible to be efficient unless you have a desk or table, some sort of shelving and a filing cabinet or box of some kind.

- The space closest to where you sit is your most valuable – guard it like precious jewels. Make sure that the things you use constantly are close enough for you to reach without having to stand up or stretch very far. And don't let space-stealers with low value sneak in!
- Position your desk so you don't have to eyeball passers-by. If necessary, position a tall plant where it creates a visual barrier.
- Make sure your chair is not only comfortable, but also ergonomically correct. Who needs a bad back caused by bending over a computer for hours?
- Aim to have one place only for each item or category, with the possible exception of backup supplies. (For example, stationery.)

Desks

Everyone, from senior executives to homemakers and students, functions better if they have a space they can set up for their personal use. If you're on the road a lot and work extensively on your laptop, you still need a place back at base to store any paperwork, regular stationery, files and relevant equipment.

Desk designs vary greatly but for many of us the most convenient configurations either have one or two drawers and a file drawer, maybe a mobile storage unit tucked underneath or beside the desk, and possibly nearby shelves, tables or cupboards to place things we use constantly.

Standing desks are becoming very popular. Some experts have gone as far as to say that sitting is the new smoking – that if we stand at least some of the day to work we will keep better health.

Filing equipment comes in many styles

The main ones are:

1. Step files. These clever little gadgets aren't for all your paperwork. Rather, they're designed to hold your constantly needed 'in regular use' paper activity. One of my course participants designed the best example I've seen, the very attractive Quefile. Its special feature is that it's light to carry and folds down for postage. I keep mine close by but not in direct eye range. You'll see it illustrated in our shopping cart at www.gettingagrip.com/product/quefile-the-desk-clutter-solution/

2. Cardboard or wooden filing boxes to hold suspension files. These can be kept in a cupboard, or under or near your desk. Open-topped file racks on wheels do a similar job. They work well if you don't have a lot of materials to manage.

3. Desks with one file drawer. Also sufficient for people with low volume.

4. Traditional vertical filing cabinets with two, three or four pull-out drawers. They hold cardboard suspension folders and are excellent if you have quite a bit of information to file, space is not at a premium and usually only one person at a time needs to use them.

5. Lateral cabinets. Although the most expensive, this is the most efficient method for large organisations. More than one person can access them at a time, they work on a colour-coded filing system which makes misfiling significantly harder and they take up less footprint than the traditional vertical files because there are no drawers to pull out. However, their coding system is more complex and takes longer to set up. You need an index. Unless you have experienced staff who've worked with lateral systems before, it's best to hire the supplier to do the initial setup.

6. Top retrieval drawer systems. If space is at a premium, these are the best option. They're similar to upright vertical cabinets but take up a lot less space than the other methods described, due to their design and the very light-weight cardboard filing stationery. They're easy to use. One brand is Tidy Files, available in South Africa and Australia. There are variations in other countries – do an online search.

CLEARING UP THE CLUTTER – HOW TO BECOME A CHAOS BUSTER

Be prepared to have fun and enjoy the task in hand. You're going to feel great when it's done. Your goal is to eliminate the mess from your work station and feel in control of your environment and your work.

Necessary equipment:

1. As discussed above, a desk, shelves and the appropriate filing system for your needs.
2. Plenty of drop files, label holders and labels if working with traditional filing systems. If you choose one of the upright systems, the company who sells it to you will provide the necessary equipment.
3. A bundle of manila folders. (Get the coloured ones if you like a colourful office.)
4. Plenty of rubbish sacks! You might need to order in a secure destruction bin.
5. A bundle of periodical or pamphlet boxes. You want your stored items to stand up rather than lie flat in an unruly pile, just waiting to escape. If you're not sure what periodicals boxes are, go into your nearest library and see how they store pamphlets, magazines and other more ephemeral materials. The beauty of these little treasures is that you can store small skinny items and loose pieces of paper upright. By using some of your brightly coloured manila folders you can also create sub-categories within your pamphlet boxes.
6. Have some cardboard document boxes for storage of archival material such as accounts or correspondence of previous years. Whether you need foolscap size or the big boxes that hold three foolscap boxes depends on what and how much you need to archive.

A basic rule of storage: where possible store things upright, even document boxes and books. As soon as you have to shift something off a heap to get at an item further down, you're inviting trouble. Nothing will go back exactly where it came from. Also, it takes more time to reach a box at the bottom of a pile so you're more likely to delay putting things away.

Another vital rule is to label everything clearly. If you change the contents you can always put a new sticker on the box. If you're reluctant to label something in case you have to relabel it, write in pencil.

Plan of attack:

1. Depending on the state and size of your office, you may need anything from an hour or two to a whole day. Dedicate uninterrupted time to the task. Don't take phone calls or accept meetings – the objective is to stay focused and get completion on the day, if at all possible.

2. Start with the top of the desk. Pile everything into a pile (or several if necessary). Handle each piece of paper. Throw out any obviously obsolete material. With the rest, sort into broad categories on the floor – there's usually not enough space anywhere else. E.g.: Bank Statements; Property; Tax; Marketing; Business Development; Legal.

3. As you create each pile, write the topic on a piece of paper and place it so it protrudes from underneath the heap. You can then identify at a glance (while you're still sorting) what the heaps are.

4. Make a separate pile of stationery, envelopes, stamps, pens, and any other miscellaneous items. Another two piles will be (a) to take home and (b) to return (or give) to others.

5. Put anything that needs immediate action aside, to attend to after you've finished. Unless it's a crisis, do *not* get side-tracked into action now or you'll end up in a worse pickle.

6. When the desk top is clear, repeat the process with the drawers, then the rest of the room except the filing cabinet. (Most people will be too mentally exhausted to confront decisions about archival filing materials on the same day.)

7. Be ruthless with the rubbish. There is almost always a worse magpie than you whom you can rely on to be the company hoarder! As you touch each item, constantly ask yourself:
   - Do I need this?
   - When was the last time I looked at it?
   - What is the worst thing that will happen if I don't have it?
   - Does anyone else have another copy?
   - Is the information online or somewhere else that I can access?

8. Don't be side-tracked into reading all the old stuff at this point. You are only sorting it. If you want to closely examine something before deciding its fate, make a heap of *To Read*

Later or *To Do*. If you find those two heaps have 90 percent of your paper, you're not being tough enough on yourself and may need some help.

9. Work quickly. If you're not very self-disciplined, ask a neat-freak friend or colleague to work with you. Get them to ask you the questions above if you start side-tracking. I've often taken this 'stand-over' role with clients; every one of them has commented that, if they hadn't had help they would have maintained momentum for about fifteen minutes and then been distracted into some interesting little by-way. The allotted time would have vanished and they would have been in a worse mess. It's more fun with someone else too, if tidying-up isn't your favourite activity.

10. Once every drawer, shelf and cupboard is completely empty and the broad categories are sorted it's time for a deeper cull and then to find places for everything. Do not do this until every item has been placed in a labelled pile. Now, and only now, start putting things back. If you begin sooner you'll end up putting useful things on top of old junk, just perpetuating the clutter and never clearing your head.

11. A lot of material has already gone into the rubbish sacks but now you fine-tune each heap as you place it in its final home. Keeping uppermost in your mind the questions at Point 7, handle each item. Again, remember, you are not thoroughly reading everything – you're just skimming to check that you (a) need to keep this item, and (b) that you're putting it in the right place. Be ruthless.

12. A nice touch is to arrange books on the shelves alphabetically by author or by subject (unless you've only got a handful). Return those that have 'accidently' forgotten to wend their way back to their rightful owners. (There speaks an ex-librarian!)

13. With paper to go in the filing cabinet, think, '*In a month's time, where would I be likely to look for this?*'. If it's equipment, the question is, '*How often do I use this, and where is it going to be most useful?*'. If it's something you use regularly, how about putting it in a nearby drawer? Never have frequently-used items more than an arm's-reach away.

14. As you place material in files, label each file.

I encourage people to have as little clutter as possible on top of their desks. Have you ever felt that there isn't much space on your desk to work? It may be the work waiting to grab you round the throat and we'll deal with that soon. Or is it because the ruler, eraser, stapler, paper-punch, paper-clips, piles of dusty cards, three coffee-cups and your lunch, as well as other miscellaneous equipment, are taking up most of your desk-top?

One caution – the way you set up your desk and office partly relies on the type of mind you have. The more linear organised people like their things systematic, convenient, logically placed, and probably out of sight; creative folk like the stimulation of brightly coloured things around them, visual, in sight. Both are right – mess is not!

We're finished being Chaos Busters, but we have to know how to handle new material as it deluges us.

HOW WE CONCENTRATE — A CRITICAL FACT

Before we continue with the next stage – how to set up your desk – it's time to share a very important piece of information about the way we concentrate.

When working manually with paper of any sort, the attention span of most people is about twenty minutes – if they don't have other external interruptions.

Our attention goes in a wave pattern. At the beginning of the task we can concentrate fully and are unlikely to interrupt ourselves. However, as the minutes tick by, the chance of self-interruptions increases. If you have multitudes of distractions waving hands at you in the form of all those other pieces of paper on your desk, it becomes increasingly difficult to maintain total focus on what you're doing. Suddenly another item has distracted you and before you know it, you're off on some unrelated errand. This is why every time management specialist says: *'Keep your desk clear of all but what you're working on'*. By doing so you hugely reduce the chance of distractions.

Working with computers is the exception to the rule. I think it's something to do with the way we interact with computers. Our mind, our eyes, and our hands are engaged and the screen constantly changes.

Most will agree that we have a much greater attention span when working with a keyboard and screen.

SETTING UP GOOD SYSTEMS

If you've got a top drawer, this is a great place to keep the tools you need all the time. Throw out the chewing gum, broken sunglasses, spare packs of staples for the stapler you lost two years ago and those obsolete bus tickets. Remember, the space closest to you is precious.

Some people prefer to keep their tools on top of their desk. You have to decide whether the fraction of a second it takes to open and reach into your neat and tidy top drawer justifies the free space you'll create and the extra working room you'll have on top of your desk. I believe it does, but as I mentioned above, you may prefer a visual display.

If you've got a second drawer, that's a good spot for more bulky things such as electronic equipment, spare business cards, maybe even your lunch.

The file drawer, if you've got one, is where you keep the regular files you need to access, suspended from their rail. But – I've seen a *lot* of bottom drawers with obsolete junk, whisky, chocolate biscuits, running gear, handbags – everything but working files. A terrible waste of important space!

Examples of possible categories in your file drawer:
- Long-term projects that you often work on.
- Staff files. (If you have to store anything confidential, some file drawers have keys.)
- A 'Half-way to File 13' file (alias the rubbish bin). This is hugely useful. It holds the items that don't justify filing, but which you're not ready to throw out just yet. These could include printing jobs waiting to be checked when a proof comes back from the type-setter, newsletters and so on. It makes a great safety net. Occasionally you'll have reason to look for something there. When you do, throw out anything obviously obsolete. You'll find the file never gets too fat.

In- and out-trays – traps for the unwary!
We'd better talk about in- and out-trays here. Many people have them

in pride of place on their desks, breeding prodigiously.

First of all, why do you need an out-tray? If you're scrupulous about keeping it empty, good on you, but people have all kinds of treasures languishing there. You probably don't need one.

Here's a little trick to make out-trays obsolete. (I learnt it when a busy mother of six small children and had to simplify or I'd sink under the house-work. As I worked in one room, anything which belonged elsewhere was put near the door so that I could take it with me the next time I went in that direction.) At my desk, when I finish with any item, I place it on the floor beside my chair. The next time I stand up, I put whatever is on the floor in its proper home. This includes filing paper in the cabinet. Exceptions are: when the archival storage is some distance away, you're in a large firm with filing clerks, or if you're a senior executive with an assistant to handle the filing.

There are many benefits. There's never any material waiting for a 'spare' moment. Everything is put away while it's still fresh in your mind, which saves time refamiliarising yourself later, and your office is always tidy (except for the small number of items on the floor around your chair if you haven't stood up for a little while). Plus, there's more room on your desk.

If an out-tray does work for you, place it so it's not distracting and empty it every time you stand up.

Are you using your in-tray correctly?
If you've got an in-tray, position it either outside your line of vision or behind you. Do be careful though; the temptation is for all manner of miscellaneous items to snuggle in. The correct use for an in-tray is to hold items that have just arrived, not to be a long-term parking lot for things you can't make a decision on, or a cosy residential address for a quiet family of mice. The critical action is to *make a decision as to location* the first time you handle something. When you're taking a break from another task, quickly sort and re-locate whatever's in your tray, following the Decision-Making method coming up next. If others are in the habit of dumping on your desk, either train yourself to reposition their gifts, or train them!

Help! Where is that piece of paper?

In case you haven't yet got the message about little bits of paper – kill them! They're a major trap. Just ask a confirmed note maker if they've ever lost a vital piece of paper. I promise you – they have. Instead, write any notes in your diary or journal. If you've got two pages to a day, you have plenty of room to record phone numbers, key points of conversations and any other information that would have formerly decorated scrappy bits of paper. Or, use a notebook/journal. Much better than rummaging through the rubbish bin!

KEY POINT No. 29: *Out-of-control paper is like a stone thrown in a pool — the ripples affect those around.*

MAINTAINING THE SYSTEMS SO YOU DON'T FALL BACK INTO CHAOS

We've got the systems sorted out, but now we have to keep them running smoothly. Let's look at how to maintain it.

We struggle daily with an ever-flowing river of paper. Relax, there are only four basic things you can do with any piece of paper or digital information. Catch a **RAFT** to keep you floating. If you don't, you'll drown.

- **Read**
- **Act**
- **File**
- **Throw**

Here are a few quick pointers for each function.

READ

- Learn to skim read.
- Don't read things you won't remember.
- Reduce (or eliminate) items that are just time fillers, other than topics of personal interest.
- Cancel magazines and papers you don't have time to read.
- Create a reading file for the times you have to wait for someone or something. Never go anywhere without a back-up activity (even the fish and chip shop).

- How many hours a month do you spend in the bathroom? Have a pile of useful reading material in there.
- Take a rapid reading course.
- Read non-fiction books like you read newspapers. Even if you only skim one non-fiction title per week, and take away just a few key points, you'll be way ahead of your opposition.
- If it's your book, use a highlighter.
- Plan regular reading times in your schedule.

ACT

The reason many people don't want to change the habit of keeping work on top of the desk is that they're scared they'll lose sight of important things if they're placed in a drawer, a filing cabinet, or a folder. Quite right, unless they're following the next recommendation. The answer is not *doing* the actual work but in making rapid and effective decisions about where to put things.

Today's Paperwork = Decisions Needed

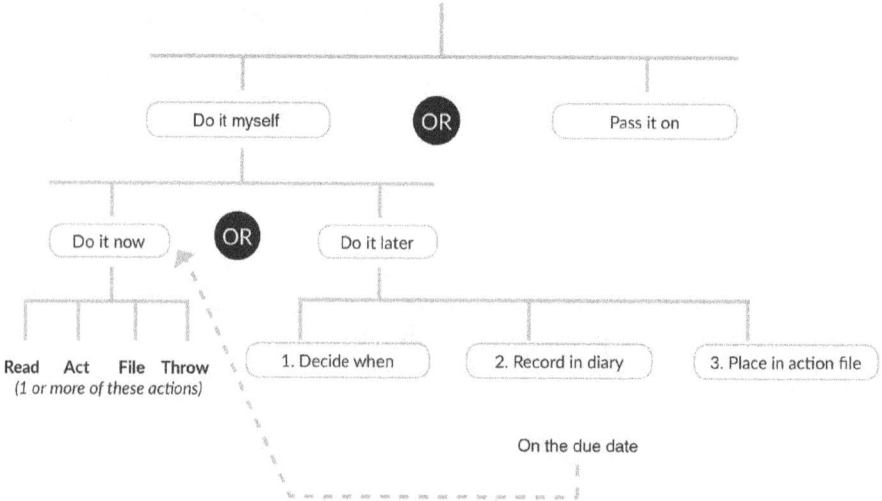

Do it myself   OR   Pass it on

Do it now   OR   Do it later

Read   Act   File   Throw
(1 or more of these actions)

1. Decide when   2. Record in diary   3. Place in action file

On the due date

The Decision-Making Matrix

The first two choices are - *Do It Myself* or *Pass It On*. From there the next simple decision is *Do It Now* or *Do It Later*. If it's *Do It Now* you'll immediately do one or more of the four activities –Read, Act, File and/ or Throw.

The deciding question is *Can I deal with this in less than two or three minutes?* If so, you'll want to action it almost immediately. If not, put it in a *Do It Later* pile. If it's *Do it Later,* as you see in the diagram, there are three steps, none of them optional.

1. Decide when you need to do the work
2. Record in your diary, on the day you need to start the project, not when it's due. If you might forget where you've filed it, note that in the diary also.
3. Now you can safely put it out of sight in the appropriate file. It might be in your Quefile or your bottom file drawer, or even in a dedicated space on a shelf but *not* on your desk. It won't emigrate, nor will it vanish. You don't have to worry about it again until the appropriate day (as long you check your diary daily). Instead you can work on today's priorities with an uncluttered mind.

When action time comes around, you're back to one or more of the four basic activities.

FILE

Everything you keep costs you time and money. Around 85 percent of what we file is never looked at again and yet many organisations spend huge amounts of money on storage, sometimes erecting special buildings. The emphasis should be on retention of useful information plus efficient retrieval, keeping what only what's *really* needed, not just mindlessly storing paper.

Day-to-day filing is a task that many would prefer to dodge. Why do we file things? Is it really a clerical function? I believe that, in general, filing is best done by the person who generates the paper and that might include the boss. Why?

- The person who works with the paper is in the best position to know where to put it when finished.
- They're already familiar with the contents.
- If they've put something away they're more likely to remember where it is when needed.
- If the assistant is away, the person needing it isn't held up, not knowing where to look.

Information is a valuable strategic resource. The harder it is to locate, the less valuable it is.

Some tips that might help:

- About every six – twelve months, have a purge of your filing cabinets. Appoint a day for the whole company to do the same task (and organise a rubbish collection or a shredder for the next day!).
- Decide on a labelling system that works for you – the simpler the better. It could be alphabetical, numerical, geographic, colour coded, by date or a combination of a couple of systems. Alpha is the most popular. Label by starting with the broadest category first, the reverse of how we address an envelope, and keep breaking down to smaller headings, e.g. Properties/Maintenance/Contractors.
- If the person receiving the mail writes the file name on at time of reading, it doesn't have to be read again in order to decide where to file it.
- If more than one person is using the system, a cross-reference list may help. Don't go overboard on this, though. Keep it brief. You're not trying to catalogue a library here. If you're using a numerical system, you will also need an index posted in some obvious place.
- Don't use paper-clips to clip papers together. Staple.
- There's nothing worse than a filing cabinet you can't get your hand into. Always have enough space to move the files and easily get documents in and out.
- Try pencilling in a 'throw-by' date when you first receive something. Then you don't have to re-read the whole thing later to see whether it's obsolete.
- Beware of miscellaneous files. They become fat sticky traps with the slightest encouragement! If you have more than a dozen pieces in a miscellaneous file, something will be waiting for its own category.
- When multiple people access the files, use an out card of some kind to show that a file is away being used. What you use depends on the kind of file, but it might be a coloured card which stands out like a sore thumb and has room to write the name of the

current user. This can save a lot of frustration and wasted time for people wandering around frustrated, saying, *'Have you seen the file for...?'*

Filing archival material

There are organisations dedicated to safely storing your archival material. I strongly recommend investigating them. They handle fire, water, and security risks much better than any non-specialist ever could. They also have amazingly efficient retrieval systems which don't cost you an arm and a leg if you want material back for some reason. They'll even come in and sort out your mess, catalogue it and tell you what can be discarded and what needs to be kept. The cost is minimal compared with the value of your time, or your staff's time if they're not retrieval experts.

THROW

What stops you from throwing out your obsolete papers? Consider how you can reduce the amount of material that lands on your desk. Don't accept written information that you don't need, just to keep a salesperson happy.

What subscriptions can you cancel? One of my course participants was GM of a national branch of an international health company. He was telling the group how he received the monthly magazines from all the other national subsidiaries because they gave him good ideas for his own monthly magazine. Suddenly he stopped.

With a look of horror on his face, he said, *'I've just realised something. I can't read all the languages!'*

The next week he reported that he'd cleaned out and cancelled most of them!

Reduce

Check the forms your company uses. Almost everyone can find ways to improve them. Next time they're due for a reprint, have a company brainstorming session to question and improve. Some of the information may no longer be needed and you'll be able to reduce both questions and forms. Have a Save a Tree day.

Encourage people to do short memos and reports. Reward clarity. I love Mark Twain's pithy little phrase: *'I'm sorry I had to write you a long letter. I didn't have time for a short one.'*

We've all suffered at the hand of those who indulge in gobble-de-gook. Death to jargon! If you want a refresher course on unintelligible garbage, try reading the official reports of many government departments, some material from higher learning institutions and even the writing of some management 'experts'. Do they know that most of the world has no idea what they're talking about? Is it a form of intellectual snobbery, and if so, who's laughing at whom? It takes skill and training to write simply and clearly instead of using the fashionable language of your industry. Those who use long, flowery phrases in preference to clean, honest language show intellectual laziness and sloppy practise. If you've got the courage to do it, send such reports back to their originators and ask for a translation. The reaction could be fun!

A PLACE FOR EVERYTHING AND EVERYTHING IN ITS PLACE
That old adage again! You bet!

If you get into the habit of putting things immediately in their place instead of leaving them to tidy away later, you'll save time, energy and frustration. The people who always seem to lose glasses and keys only do so because they haven't got a regular place to put them.

This rule also applies to what you keep on and in your desk. Decide which files you want at fingertip reach and which can go in the storeroom or filing cabinet. What will you put in your file drawer, what sits on the desk and what goes in the top drawer? Those few minutes invested in thinking about your natural workflow will save hours.

ELECTRONIC SYSTEMS
I haven't spent time discussing electronic transfer and storage of data because it's a specialist field. If used correctly, there are huge savings to be made, but many of my very computerised clients tell me that if a company doesn't have good manual systems and clarity about what needs storing, electronic systems will end up being a repository for rubbish just as much as an over-flowing and unpruned old-fashioned filing cabinet. My recommendation is – know clearly what you need

and then talk to the people using electronic systems. Ask around. Find the people who are happy with the systems they use. Don't just rely on the so-called experts. If you can't understand what they're telling you, do some more homework until you do. You could waste a huge amount of time and money setting up systems which don't do what you want.

FINAL POINTERS ON KEEPING CONTROL OF YOUR INFORMATION

- Develop a 'do it now' mentality.
- Always ask yourself — does this item have enough value to warrant the time, money, and energy required to save it?
- Imagine you have an invisible silver cord connecting you to every possession. Does it energise you or emotionally drain you?
- The principles of managing paper apply to electronic information management as well. Clear out your clutter, set up good systems (folders in your computers), label everything, delete things you don't need now, archive old versions of documents into named sub-folders.
- For a much more in-depth coverage of the office setup and paper and information management, check out my *Getting a Grip on the Paper War.* I wrote it because so many people asked for more than I have space to give in this general overview of time management.

Remember – we're all human. Don't beat yourself up if sometimes you slip back into old ways – it takes time to change. No matter how perfectly you set up this system there will still be times when you feel as if the dump-truck has called by!

I do promise, however, that if you practise you will eventually gain an awesome amount of power over your daily work and you'll use your time far more effectively. Until I learnt the techniques I've described, I used to be a great little collector and my desk was regularly messy. The main reason was the lack of a system. Once I mastered keeping materials off my desk until I was ready to work on them, with the confidence that they wouldn't disappear into a black hole, it was six months before my files needed a sort-out. Since then, a tidy desk has become a habit, like brushing my teeth. It feels uncomfortable when it's got more than one task on it.

CHAPTER 12 PROCRASTINATION – THE ENERGY-SUCKER

What is procrastination? The art of putting off until tomorrow that which could, and should, be done today.

If something needs doing, why leave it until another day? Will it get any easier? Procrastination is the enemy of your success.

At every speech I give on time management, there are always people who put their hands up for this particular challenge. Those who suffer from it understand very well the earlier discussions about living under pressure, dashing from Frenetic to Reactive behaviour. They quietly hope that the Proactive items will be swallowed in quick-sand, for they never seem to get around to them! The sufferers of the Big P always have a slightly harried look about them, as if invisible sheep-dogs were nipping at their heels, pushing them into places they don't want to be in.

The best way to stop procrastination is never to start it! Effective planning is the best way I know to overcome this problem. After all these years of helping people with their time management habits it still surprises me how many people talk about what they want to do but don't actually plan their projects or the allocation of their time resources. They're not placing a high value on every minute. Result: they waste many hours a week. The more time you spend on planning, the less you will need to complete tasks, the better your results and the more time you'll have for fun and pleasure.

Have you ever seen a laser show, possibly at a big stage production or a civic display? Think of the intensity and power with which laser beams cut through the air. They don't waver about. Learn to develop 'laser thinking' – it will save you from procrastination.

How do you feel when you know you've delayed yet again on attempting something that, in your heart, you know you had a good chance of succeeding at? Do you feel good, effective, and pleased with yourself? Of course the answer is 'no'. Sticking at a task until completed to the necessary standard is a mark of character.

IMPROVE YOUR ABILITY TO PRIORITISE

Many people struggle with the balance between the urgent and the important.

- Did Chapters 4 and 5 resonate with you? Keep focusing on Proactive activities. If you plan your work on a weekly basis, followed by daily review, I promise that you *will* beat procrastination. Just think how much progress you'll make in a year if you improve by even one percent each week in each important activity.
- Work your daily tasks in order of their priority, as described in Chapter 6. Then the most important things *will* be done first. This will often be something you'd otherwise procrastinate on.
- In addition, every time you feel yourself losing focus, ask yourself my favourite question: *'What is the best use of my time right now?'* Develop a sense of urgency. Try setting an artificial deadline.

THE POWER OF WRITTEN GOALS

Typically, procrastinators are not good goal-setters. Unless we have a clear written and/or visual picture of what we want to achieve and when, we tend to float gently through life in a wishful haze of *'one day soon'*, and *'I'll get round to it later'*. Be clear about what you want to achieve. The best goals have a clearly defined outcome. To help you visualise your future success, ask yourself:

- What is the end result?
- What will it look like when finished?
- What are the quickest ways to achieve the result?

Don't just have the goals wandering around your head. Write them down. In all my years of research and reading, I have not come across anyone who succeeded greatly without initially tapping into the power of writing down and visualising their goals. It unleashes the secret power of focus.

Have deadlines but – beware of being unrealistic. Trying to reach impossible deadlines is very de-motivating and won't help you break the procrastination habit.

Sub-divide your tasks into the smallest possible action steps, with achievable time-lines. Set target dates on each specific action. Then, every time you finish a small step there's a sense of goal achievement. This helps to get you started and builds your belief that you can achieve something.

Before you start each day, overview what you did the day before. You'll quickly realise if you're trying to achieve too much too quickly. It's okay to take longer if necessary. Many people give up on goal-setting because they miss deadlines. Here's a hint. Every goal-setter has missed some! Don't give up. Just re-schedule the time or increase the activity rate and keep going.

Beware of just doing maintenance work when you have a big project you want to complete. For instance, you may want to create a new garden while still keeping the rest of your section or yard tidy. The temptation is to do a general tidy-up first, because you'll get a quick result. If you do, it's very likely you'll never get started on the big project because of interruptions. There's enormous satisfaction when you're self-determined enough to say 'no' to the easy task and instead, make a start on the big task. Your self-esteem is enlarged because you've been strong-willed enough to make bold time decisions; the sense of forward momentum more than compensates for the short-term disorder.

There are parallel situations in business. Alarm bells ring when I hear someone say *'I'm just going to* ... (some low-level task) *before I start on* ...' (a high-value activity). I can almost guarantee that they've got a blockage (for one reason or another) about starting a more important activity. Develop the habit of moving forward on activities that will, in the long-term, make a permanent difference. For example, if you're a salesperson with a messy desk, push the mess to one side so it doesn't distract you and spend half-an-hour doing five prospecting calls. Or you're a student with exams looming and your bedroom's a tip. Put in some solid study first. Then go back and tidy the room.

KEY POINT No. 30: *Don't focus on the immediate at the expense of the permanent.*

BE A SELF-STARTER

Some people have difficulty moving from planning to doing. The only way to overcome that problem is to start, even if it is only a small action step – just start somewhere. Once you have all the facts, get moving. If there is something that you seem unable to get to, re-examine it. Does it really have to be done? If not, cross it off the list – it is only de-motivating to keep looking at it. If it is important, stop mucking around and do *something*. Find a beginning task (sometimes known as a leading task) that will get you moving.

- You might start a work project by assembling all the necessary paperwork on your desk. Or tell your secretary or colleagues that you're not available for an hour. You may have to shift your work to a different location.
- If you're procrastinating on getting the accounts ready for the accountant, make an appointment far enough ahead that you have time to prepare. This will push you into preparation mode.
- If you don't want to go to the dentist, don't think about the actual visit and what it entails. Just pick up the phone and make the appointment. The rest takes care of itself, once the first action is done.
- A decision to get fit might be moved into action by ringing a friend to go running together.

Many years ago I wanted to have a major sort-out of my files. It involved combining the contents of two cabinets and removing the smaller one. This was going to make more room in my study and help me be more efficient. It must be something to do with my early working years as a librarian, but I actually enjoy sorting paperwork and creating a smooth-running system! However, over the years I've trained myself to spend quality business hours on income-generating activities, rather than having fun doing re-organising. Therefore, I decided to treat myself with this cabinet declutter project over the next holiday weekend. The tricky bit was that, once the weekend arrived, it was very difficult to start. Everyone around me was having a holiday. My subconscious started to rebel; a delicious novel beckoned.

I had to trick myself to get started. I pulled out files and started putting things into heaps (the leading task). I made such a big mess that I knew I couldn't bear to walk past the door and look at it all weekend. And then I kept going a little longer, until there was a sense of progress. Past experience said that once I got beyond the initial pain of starting, it would be pleasurable and satisfying. Then I knew I could trust myself to complete the job as quickly as possible. It was finished in a few hours! That book was a lovely reward!

VISUALISE THE COMPLETED TASK

Most procrastinators are unable to see themselves completing the task they're stuck on. If you haven't got a clear mental picture in your 'necktop computer' of what you want to achieve, you have much less chance of achieving it. Every house built, every thriving business, every top sports achievement starts in someone's mind.

Visualisation is very powerful. It's as if you're playing a video in your mind. Here's a simplified version of what I learned from Shakti Gawain's *Creative Visualisation* (mentioned in Chapter 3) and the key to my getting off welfare.

1. Decide what you want to achieve.
2. Picture yourself achieving each step of the project with ease and excellence.
3. Imagine these images are your 'Success video'.
4. Spend a few minutes relaxing, slowing your mind down.
5. Play your 'Success video' on your internal TV screen. Use all five of your senses. In your imagination see, smell, touch, hear and taste successful outcomes.
6. Do it daily, for about five minutes (or more if you can). No-one becomes good at anything in one short burst. We don't become fit after two or three trips to the gym, or good salespeople after two observations of another experienced person. Practise is the key ingredient to permanent success.

If you want to give an excellent presentation, see yourself in front of the client or group, being successful. Imagine how good you'll feel when the client says 'yes', or when the group has adopted your ideas. See them sitting forward, interested in what you're saying, nodding their heads. Hear their enthusiastic comments about your recommendations. Feel the positive atmosphere in the room.

You want to improve a relationship. See yourself talking harmoniously with your friend as you look out the window of your favourite restaurant. Imagine how the meal tastes. Smell the aromas coming from the kitchen. Feel the positive flow of energy as you engage in stimulating conversation. Hear the laughter between the two of you.

If it's a sports achievement, see yourself playing perfect strokes, or making top scores. Hear the crowd roar as you make a brilliant play. Feel the power pumping through your fit body. Smell the grass, or any other distinctive aroma.

If you can visualise success, you'll be much more likely to do the necessary work. Practise visualising things you might otherwise postpone and you'll find you achieve much more, with far less procrastination.

YOUR PHYSICAL ENVIRONMENT

There are a number of things you can do physically to overcome procrastination. The conditions you work in can aggravate it. For example, if you're too hot or too cold you'll struggle to concentrate. What will help you achieve top productivity? (Note: your answers might be different from those around you.) Observe the noise levels, amount of light and time of day in which you function best. Do you work better alone or with others, before or after strenuous exercise? Are you a fowl (up with the pre-dawn roosters) or an owl who doesn't function in top gear until later in the day and into the evening? Seek a work environment that encourages you to action.

Take a short walk to clear your mind if you're getting stuck. New ideas will come from the sights, sounds and smells you experience and you'll return much fresher to your task.

Maybe it's just exhaustion that blocks you from getting cracking on a big task. If you're really tired, it may be that your body is sending you a message. Instead of fighting it, give yourself permission to notice the tiredness and do something about it. You'll recover much faster. A tired person is like a car with no petrol – no can go! (See the next chapter for a discussion on power naps.)

OVERCOME INDECISION

Sometimes we dither around, not knowing which of several mutually exclusive activities to do. At this point it's helpful to re-examine our priorities.

Have you ever been given an invitation to do something you'd enjoy, or that seems a good idea, but in your heart of hearts you know you can't do it justice? When you analyse your time commitments, you realise you have to make a choice. Your long-term goals will help you make the 'right' decision, which is how we started this book. The longer you toy with the tantalising alternatives, the longer you justify and try to trick your intuition, the more muddled and confused you become.

There's a huge release of power once the right decision is made. You get back on track and stop procrastinating on the activities that really matter. To help find the 'right' decision, ask yourself *'Where or how will I get the best long-term results, congruent with my goals and values?'* Another filter question which I find valuable is *'What lights me up?'*

Every day brings good opportunities. The power is in making the *best* choices. Think of people you admire greatly and ask yourself: *'Would ... spend their time on this task, if they had my goals?'* Practise listening to your intuition. Most importantly, make the decision quickly and then move on. Don't vacillate.

COMMITMENT

Once you've made a decision, if you share your goal with someone supportive you'll be much more likely to complete. Give another person permission to monitor you, make yourself answerable to them and watch how committed you'll become, not to mention the progress you'll make.

When a single mother on welfare (many years ago now) I decided to train for a modified marathon (24 km or 15 miles). A number of my running friends were competing and challenged me to participate. I'd never run that distance and really didn't think I could do it. However, once I made the decision and shared it with them, they became a vital element in the outcome. I'm absolutely sure there was no way I would have sustained the three-month training programme without them.

Because I'd given them permission to check and coach me, they had a personal interest in supporting me; they were committed to my success. The combined energy, commitment and focus of us all was enough to propel me through the old internal conversations about being (a) too slow, (b) too heavy, (c) not fit enough, and (d) not having enough time. The old excuses dropped away, powerless to stop me. I didn't need them anymore. For that time, at least, procrastination was conquered.

The benefits from taking part in that race far exceeded the buzz I got from completing in a much better time than estimated. At the time both my work situation and the relationship I was in were rather negative. The increase in self-esteem because I'd persevered with my training regime and the newly trim body gave a great boost of confidence. It was a major factor in having enough self-belief to move on to new horizons, new people and the wonderful life I now lead.

When you make a commitment to others you'll think less about yourself and more about them. Your desire to keep the good opinion of people you respect is more powerful than your own fears and indecisions. And when others share your accomplishments and cheer you on, progress is sweet.

Once you establish a habit, and 21-28 days is enough to get a base laid, it really doesn't require anywhere near as much effort to keep going. The hardest part is about three to four days after you've started the new activity. Alerting someone else to check you at that time, before you get there and feel like giving up, is a big help to breaking through the barrier.

BUILD MOTIVATION

Many people procrastinate because of lack of motivation; if you're not motivated you won't use your time well. You'll constantly find yourself spending time in Reactive and Time-Wasting activities.

From there it's very easy to keep spiralling downwards into more and more inefficiencies. If you're feeling down or sorry for yourself, seek positive, encouraging people to associate with. Remove yourself from regular association with negative people. Your mental state requires good food, just like your body. Only the recipes are different.

Think of a lake, wrapped in the folds of the surrounding hills. It's fed by the water running off the hills after rain, little streams flowing in and maybe a spring nearby. Imagine another stream flowing away from this lake. If, over time the water flowing out is more than the water running in, in due course the lake turns into a mud hole. So it is with our minds. Negative thought is a drain on our energy and our ability to function effectively. It diminishes rather than enlarges us. If we allow in more negative influences than positive, the glory of our minds becomes a bog-hole of depression, negativity, and limited thinking.

To change the ratios:
- Identify what is negative and what positive.
- Make sure that there's at least 51 percent positive input going into our heads on a daily basis. Anything above 51 percent is going to move us on to success in our lives, slowly but surely. As we move forward, so the habit of procrastination drops away.

Creating a positive input means eliminating, or least reducing, the things, events and people who drain us. Cut down on negative reading in books, magazines, newspapers and social media. Stop watching negative programmes. Don't start the day by listening to the world's disasters. If you don't hear every news programme you'll still know what's going on in the world – someone will tell you anything important! Don't go to bed with a nightcap of the news or screen violence. Let the last thoughts of the day be positive ones. Give your sub-conscious productive challenges to work on while you sleep. Treat boring, whinging, negative people as if they have the plague. They do. They suffer from a deadly, life-sucking disease called *it's not fair* – more insidious than normal diseases because it's invisible. Such people do not realise that they're 100 percent responsible for changing their own circumstances.

If you work in a negative environment, or for a negative boss, get out while you still have a mind. Why give so much of your precious time

– indeed, your life – to someone you neither like nor respect, or for a company you don't trust. Extensive research shows that happy people suffer less stress and ill-health. They live longer and have better quality of life. So, the more negative stress you live with, the shorter your life might be. Just one of the studies reviewed by University of Illinois Professor Emeritus of Psychology Ed Diener, also a senior scientist for the Gallup Organization of Princeton, N.J., followed nearly 5,000 university students for more than 40 years. It found that those who were most pessimistic as students tended to die younger than their peers.

If that isn't an important consideration about the way we use our time, what is? When people first become aware of this principle, they often say things like *'But I don't want to lose my friends.'* Relax – true friends are glad to see you get ahead and find success and happiness. As you grow, so will they. And there are many more wonderful encouraging people waiting to meet you.

OVERCOME MENTAL FATIGUE

When I talk about depression in this section, it is *not* the serious illness of depression, but those times when you feel a bit low and dispirited and can't seem to get motivated. Someone with severe depression needs skilled help. Often low-level depression is a symptom of severe procrastination; you feel overwhelmed by the size and complexity of the task and wish it would go away. The further behind you get and the closer to an increasingly impossible deadline (because you've mucked around!) the more helpless you feel.

The following pointers may help you to overcome those feelings when they arise:
- Spend some quiet time every day. Observe the things around you. Take time to see, smell, hear and touch nature. Learn to be aware of things other than your busyness.
- Study something. Develop a mindset that says, *'Today I will learn something new.'* Every person you talk to, every book or magazine you pick up, has something to offer. Practise looking for it.
- Start something – anything that requires initiative and imagination. It's always the thinking-about-starting that bogs

people down. Once you begin, the pain vanishes and you find yourself saying, *'Why did I take so long?'*.

- Finish something, especially a Proactive activity (see Chapter 4). The power of completion is amazing. Even a very small task, once finished, causes an adrenalin flow which creates a positive charge. Every little building block of positivity helps to break down a lack of motivation and low self-esteem.
- Prioritise. Do I need to tell you again to prioritise? *Just do it!*
- Indulge your creativity. Juliet was having trouble staying focused on the secondary family business she'd committed to help her husband with. She was caught up in 'ought tos' and 'shoulds' and becoming more and more depressed. She's a very clever craftswoman who loves creating beautiful things but had put her personal interests to one side out of a sense of duty. She found that giving herself permission to go back to her quilting from time to time lifted her spirits amazingly. (We all need to express our creativity in some way; repressing it for too long kills the spirit within us.) Once she recognised this and allowed herself some regular creative time, the other important activities didn't seem so hard. She then started to achieve in those areas again.

ACKNOWLEDGE YOUR GIFTS

Write a list of all your strengths and achievements, the good things you do for other people; the ways you contribute. For many of us, feelings of low-level depression go hand-in-hand with not feeling worthwhile. At these times we can judge ourselves much too harshly.

I encourage you to recognise how unique you are. Everyone has skills and qualities to offer others, but do you notice them? Perhaps they're so familiar to you that you take them for granted.

I had a graphic illustration of this with one of my client groups. For homework I'd asked a team to write a list of their individual strengths and achievements. The next week hardly anyone had done the exercise. Almost all of them, and they were mainly quiet non-assertive people, said that they found it highly uncomfortable to turn the telescope backwards and praise themselves for what they did well. They didn't think they were particularly good at anything and kept mentioning other people who were better.

For a moment I was stumped, but inspiration struck. Focusing on one person at a time, I asked the group to tell their colleague his or her strengths, plus anything else positive they wanted to share. One person wrote down the responses and gave them to the one in the 'hot seat'. It was very moving to sit and listen to the wonderful things they were saying to each other. The first few found it very difficult to receive praise but as we continued, the squirming stopped. The result was electrifying. By the time they finished, you could feel the power, love, and care in the room.

DEVELOP NEW HABITS

This is an excellent solution – and it requires practise and time.

Benjamin Franklin (1706-1790) gave us a wonderful example of the power of surely but steadily building better habits. He was a printer, philosopher, writer, inventor and American politician and diplomat. In his day, he was known by many as 'the wisest American'. His influence on society is still felt. For example, every wearer of bi-focal glasses thanks him, he discovered that a lightning rod would divert lightning from buildings, and the Franklin stove was a huge improvement on the inefficient fireplaces of the times.

In his Autobiography he tells how argumentative he was as a young man. Eventually he decided that greater business and personal success would be his if he put himself on a virtues improvement programme. He identified thirteen areas of his life that showed room for improvement. He figured that he wouldn't try and improve all areas at the same time – one trait per week was about as much as he could handle. He was wise. None of us can cope with too much radical change.

FRANKLIN'S THIRTEEN VIRTUES

1. **Temperance**. Eat not to dullness; drink not to elevation.

2. **Silence**. Speak not but what may benefit others or yourself; avoid trifling conversation.

3. **Order**. Let all your things have their places; let each part of your business have its time.

4. **Resolution**. Resolve to perform what you ought; perform without fail what you resolve.

5. **Frugality**. Make no expense but to do good to others or yourself; i.e., waste nothing.

6. **Industry**. Lose no time; be always employ'd in something useful; cut off all unnecessary actions.

7. **Sincerity**. Use no hurtful deceit; think innocently and justly, and, if you speak, speak accordingly.

8. **Justice**. Wrong none by doing injuries or omitting the benefits that are your duty.

9. **Moderation**. Avoid extremes; forbear resenting injuries so much as you think they deserve.

10. **Cleanliness**. Tolerate no uncleanliness in body, cloaths [C18th spelling], or habitation.

11. **Tranquillity**. Be not disturbed at trifles, or at accidents common or unavoidable.

12. **Chastity**. Rarely use venery but for health or offspring, never to dullness, weakness, or the injury of your own or another's peace or reputation.

13. **Humility**. Imitate Jesus and Socrates.

He drew up a chart and developed a recording system which he updated daily in order to track his progress. At the end of each week he stopped focusing on that week's trait and moved on to the next one. His thinking was that, even if he wasn't actively focusing on something, over a period of time he would improve on all fronts. History proved him right.

So – take your time. If the slow road to continuous improvement was good enough for Ben Franklin, it's good enough for us.

SHIFT THE FOCUS OFF YOUR WEAKNESSES

Don't dwell on them in a negative way. They'll go away if they don't get enough attention. Everyone has their share, but don't focus on them as excuses – that's a sure way to wallow in procrastination. Do you want to spend your life having a pity party, or do you want to amount to something? When you're starting a new project, focusing on your weaknesses will guarantee failure. Believe in yourself. Capitalise on your strengths and gradually weaknesses will fade into insignificance.

If you had told me, when I was a struggling single mother, that I would develop a major business around time management, let alone be writing books about it, I would have laughed very loudly! I could be guaranteed to always last-minute and I was usually late for everything except buses and planes!

So what happened to change things? I began in the training field by using one of my strengths – the ability I seem to have of encouraging people – in one-on-one sessions. It was fairly basic coaching. Eventually I realised that many of my clients were asking me for help on how to handle their time. How could I, someone who used to be abysmal at time management, have that knowledge? I now know it was because I'd focused on improving my habits, rather than accepting the previous state of affairs. Rather than giving up I'd gone on courses, read books and practised, failed, practised, failed and practised some more!

KEY POINT No. 31: *Whatever you focus on enlarges.*

AVOID MAJORING IN MINOR THINGS

Majoring in minor things is another habit of people who procrastinate.

Occasionally you will find that you've done all the higher priority tasks for the day and have time to do some 'busy' tasks. These can provide welcome relief. They might include sorting the office files, entering some data in the database or any other of the various administrative tasks that accumulate. However, if you spend time on these tasks when priority jobs are left undone, you allow procrastination to take over again. Don't be fooled by your seemingly important activities. Ask yourself honestly, *'What is the most important use of my time right now?'*

HOW TO OVERCOME FEAR

Often we fear to start something in case we fail. Procrastination is greatly reduced when we understand both the task facing us and our fears about it and prepare to deal with them.

Try these strategies:
- Do you know what you are trying to accomplish, and why? Clarity with this can be a major aid to beating fear-based procrastination.
- Thoroughly analyse a job. Do a Franklin Close (also mentioned in Chapter 7). On a sheet of paper, write on one side all the reasons you have for completing a task. On the other side list all the reasons you can think of for postponing it. Write down everything you can think of and then compare the two lists. If a task is really important you will have more reasons for doing than for delaying. Just putting all the reasons down on paper will often give you the motivation to overcome your fear and commence the necessary work.
- Once you've taught yourself to analyse each situation, study each challenge closely. Research it before you start – this will help you get going. Typically, you'll find it easier to finish a task if you know more about it. Lack of knowledge can cause apathy and fear, which then encourages procrastination. If a task is worth completing, it's worth understanding.
- Sharing knowledge with others and enlisting their help will often encourage you to persevere.

- If the task is totally objectionable, the final recourse is to exit out of the situation. In such cases, that could mean even leaving a job or ending a relationship. Make a decision based on your values and priorities, but only after careful analysis of the situation. *Do not* act hastily!

UNDERSTAND THE VALUE OF CHANGE

Some people fear success, or completion of tasks; once a job is completed, their excuses for not getting on with the next thing are gone.

Change is scary! The weekend after I'd left the security of my job and become self-employed, I suffered from anxiety attacks for the first and hopefully last time of my life. It felt as though I was teetering on the edge of a high wall with no safety harness. You simply don't know what's round the next corner.

If this is you – take comfort. Change that you engineer, by progressively moving forward, is very positive. Look back in a year or so and you'll realise you're not the same person you were – and wouldn't want to be. The pain of change is the pain of birth, the pain of growth. After you've deliberately stepped out for change and progress a few times you start looking for it, because you realise that unless you're in constant change you stagnate and eventually go backwards. Winners live constantly outside their comfort zones. I like the motto of many SAS groups around the world: *'Who dares wins'*. We're not taking on terrorists, but we are taking on our own terrors.

To be sure, change which is forced upon us is not usually much fun. However, we can transmute it to a positive outcome by looking for the positive spin-off. The former CEO of a very large national real estate chain in New Zealand told me, a year after being rather dramatically dumped, that although his experience was very traumatic at the time, with hindsight he saw it as very positive. He moved back into the allied field he'd previously worked in, had no more restrictive corporate duties, a less stressful life, still enjoyed good income and best of all he didn't have to spend half his life in interminable meetings! Full credit to him for finding the upside of an initially unpleasant situation.

WHERE TO START ON BIG TASKS

For many of us, it is the getting started that causes the most trouble. Different people operate in different ways, so experiment to find out which way suits you best.

There are two opposite techniques to create momentum:
- Begin on the outside.
- Begin on the inside.

The *outside to inside* people like to assemble everything first and remove the small tasks from around the fringes before they start. For instance, they find it almost impossible to start a new project when their desk is messy. The huge risk is that spending time on trivial paper-work might equal a non-start on the big job. They can solve that by moving distractions out of sight. If they're going to clean a room, they prefer to sort out all the mess before they start the vacuum cleaner. They do the little things first, such as dusting and tidying; the big task that makes the significant difference is done last. This is the way they build momentum.

The *inside to outside* people go for the jugular – they do the big tasks first and then tidy up the fringes, (if you're lucky!)

There is no right or wrong on either of these methods, as long as the job is completed to a satisfactory standard. If you stop and think about the way you operate, you'll quickly identify which sort you are.

The traps to be aware of are:
- *Outside to inside* people sometimes don't start the big task because they're so busy getting ready
- *Inside to outside* people sometimes don't complete jobs properly because the finishing details don't motivate them!

Sometimes we just have to be really tough on ourselves and set deadlines such as *'You're not going to leave the office (or turn on the video, go to bed, or ...) until you've at least started on this job!'* Most of us can delay with excellence! Creating momentum is a learned skill. Driving through that sense of sluggishness, forcing ourselves to take control of our will, is hard at first but the more we do it, the better we feel. Our self-esteem and success build. Winners are not procrastinators. (Yes, you're right, I strongly identify with this issue. I used to get excellent grades in Procrastination Class!)

WHAT TO START WITH

It's better to start with the worst, or most unpleasant, thing you have to do in the day. Often the thing that will make the most significant long-term difference is the one thing you most don't want to do. A common issue for salespeople is making prospecting calls. Confront it. Really, it will only take a few minutes to make a few calls to three or four new prospects; the huge benefit to your self-esteem and energy far outweighs the discomfort. Over time, you become de-sensitised to the pain. One day you'll be delighted to find that you now enjoy the task that used to be hard. I speak from vast experience here, too!

Develop a *Do it now* mentality.

REWARDS

Rewards really help in the fight against procrastination. Choose a simple reward system. Try different things until you find something that really hits your hot button. It might be sleeping in on a Saturday, having a night out, giving yourself permission to sloth off for a few hours or reading a novel instead of a non-fiction book. Perhaps a points or bonus system will work for you.

> One of my first clients decided that she wanted to improve on her exercise programme. She set a goal to walk for at least half an hour three times per week. She then drew up a habit chart, (an abbreviated version of Benjamin Franklin's virtues list), and every time she took her walk, a star went up on the chart. At the end of each month she chose a reward and sometimes I was included! One month we went to the movies in the middle of the afternoon. It felt so decadent and delicious!

Two important details:
- Reward yourself only when you earn it.
- If you earn a reward, be sure to take it.

Reward systems only work if you strictly adhere to them. If you tell yourself you will stop after a certain amount of activity, or take a particular reward after achieving specific results and then don't, the motivating power of a reward diminishes.

Remember, you're dealing with the hidden giant of your sub-conscious here. If you keep saying one thing and doing another, eventually your sub-conscious digs its stubborn heels in and says 'shove off'. You will have created an internal lack of integrity. In a humorous way, I see the sub-conscious as a child. Tell your sub-conscious something for long enough (an affirmation) and it will eventually believe you. Don't keep your promises, even to yourself, however, and you've got trouble! (For more on the subject of affirmations, read Shakti Gawain's *Creative Visualisation* or John Kehoe's *Mind Power*, or Napoleon Hill's *Think and Grow Rich.*

It is much more effective to reward than punish. Writing this section reminded me of a parenting experience. One of my younger sons, aged nine at the time, had developed the unlovely habit of moaning and complaining every time I asked him to do any task.

Refrains like: *'It's not fair; it's Maurice's turn; I didn't make the mess; I don't want to,'* echoed round the house. In the midst of my frustration, one day I realised I'd begun to sound as cranky as him.

In desperation I suddenly remembered hearing about Positive Parenting. In a nutshell, if you reinforce desired behaviour and ignore or give as little attention as possible to unsatisfactory behaviour, the bad behaviour is supposed to diminish. I was clear out of ideas so decided to give it a go.

I picked a calm moment. *'Son, I'm not happy about the way you complain every time you're asked to do a chore. And I'm not happy about myself either – I'm beginning to sound like you! I've had a better idea.*

'Let's make a game of fixing it. Every time I catch you **not** *complaining when you're asked to do something, you'll get a star. We'll keep a list on the fridge. When you've earned ten stars, you get an ice cream. And if I forget to notice that you didn't complain, you're allowed to remind me. We want those stars up there as fast as possible.'*

He took up the suggestion enthusiastically and I remembered to praise him to the skies the first few times he willingly accepted a task. It was amazing how fast the habit was reinforced. After three ice creams we both forgot to keep track and it was never an issue again.

Even if you play the game just with yourself, reward the behaviour you want more of.

DEVELOP DETACHMENT

Sometimes we can be too close to a task. Get someone else to take a detached look at the situation. They will probably be able to see things you've overlooked. By explaining to someone else what your difficulties are, you'll find it easier to get a clear overview because you had to go back to basics to explain.

KNOW YOUR DEADLINES

Learn to budget time, just like any other valuable resource. Develop a tight schedule – this will help to prevent procrastination.

If you focus primarily on the 20 percent of activities that will make 80 percent of the difference, the less important activities will be crowded out. Leave undone those things that really don't matter.

WORK FAST

Sometimes a fast tempo is essential to success. Quick action creates momentum. Do you know any highly effective person who fluffs around? One man I worked for could write reports and make decisions faster than anyone else I've ever known. He wasn't always right, but he was effective more often than not, achieved heaps and had a lot of fun along the way. When you work at a fast rate, you have higher energy.

Have you ever noticed how much work you can get through when you're about to go on holiday? Tasks that have been waiting for your attention for ages suddenly get handled. You work at a higher speed. You feel powerful and effective and time flies. You leave for your holiday feeling that you've earned it. Try creating that momentum all the time. You won't achieve it very often at first, but over time it becomes a way of life and suddenly you find you're faster and more productive than those around you.

TIME FILLERS

Learn to fill the small gifts of time with useful activities. Highly effective people are minute-conscious, not hour-conscious. If we let it, work expands to fill the time available. Instead of allowing that, notice the little gaps and use them to advantage. There's sure to be something waiting for your attention. If you've already read my comments on multi-tasking in Chapter 7 you know, however, that I'm not suggesting you multi-task on anything complex.

Examples:
- Suppose you've got a few minutes before you go to lunch. Perhaps you can squeeze in a couple of quick emails, make a phone call or collect the information or supplies you need to start your next major activity.
- When you hold on the phone, put it on speaker or plug in your headset and use those moments.
- Look over the day's action plan and review the next task.
- Sort files in the gaps while waiting for calls to go through.
- Do a few press-ups or stretches while you wait for the kettle to boil.
- At home it might be cooking dinner or ironing and talking on the phone to a family member.
- Fold washing and watch a movie.
- When I was a child an aunt taught me to knit and read at the same time.

You might say you can't do simultaneous tasks. I say *'Have you tried, and persevered in your trying?'*.

(There is a gender difference. Women usually find it easier; their brains are constructed differently from men's. They have a different switching mechanism which makes it easier to handle multiple tasks concurrently. Most men, on the other hand, have the very useful ability to single-mindedly focus on one thing at a time.)

HELP FROM OTHERS FOR LARGE TASKS

If you feel overwhelmed by a task, don't be afraid to ask for help. This can move you quickly from procrastination mode to being effective.

Sometimes a task is just too big for one person but your superiors haven't recognised this. Have you told them? Make a list of all the tasks you have to do in the given time frame. Or, keep a time log for a day or two so you can show them what you're *really* doing. Until you know clearly what you're being asked to do, how can you explain the challenges to anyone else? Have some solutions when you seek help.

Don't be a martyr. If you can't do something, be prepared to say so. Sometimes the people around you are better at delegating – upwards, downwards or sideways – than you. It's human nature to keep loading a willing horse until something or someone cries halt. Our children do it, our spouses do it – why should be employers be different?

If you procrastinate on the tasks you've accepted (for whatever reason), you *and* the people around you are going to be very frustrated. It's better to let others know that you're stretched beyond capacity (or sometimes ability).

DEALING WITH OTHER PEOPLE

Be tactful and considerate of the opinions of others, but don't let their views keep you from completing your tasks. Treat everyone fairly. Come to terms with potential adversaries. Some of your worries may be unfounded but if there is conflict, try to sort it out before work starts. If you cannot get resolution, you'll just have to keep working regardless. Keep attention focused on the task, not the person. If you let your feelings about them become a reason for you to procrastinate, other people are controlling your life. Anxiety will be the result.

ONE AREA AT A TIME

Remember, don't try and change everything you're unhappy with in one go. You'll blow yourself out of the water and it's a certain guarantee for failure. Choose one area where procrastination is hurting you. Make a firm decision to deal with it, make a plan, set a deadline, find a supporter, sort out your rewards, and get started. No excuses!

KEY POINT No. 32: Nothing worthwhile comes on the first attempt.

CHAPTER 13 SANITY GAPS – ENJOY WORK LIFE BALANCE AND STILL ACHIEVE

We could be fabulous at all the elements we've talked about throughout this book but, if we don't take time out to recharge we're heading for a fall. Something will suffer – health, relationships, business or a combination of any of the three. Intellectually most of us know this; it's often discussed. But the reality for many is that they feel unable to create any real work life balance.

Before we discuss strategies to improve, let's dig a bit deeper into why so many feel their life is out of balance.

WHY *DO* WE WORK?
- Is it to provide sufficient money for food, health, a roof over your head, to pay the bills, have a little spare for some of the nice things of life and hopefully a comfortable retirement?
- You may be totally fulfilled by living a comfortable easy life, surrounded by family and friends and working in the same profession all your life.
- Maybe you have a powerful drive to rise to the top of your profession, with all the monetary advantages that suggests.
- Or philanthropy presses your buttons. You work in order to make enough money to contribute to society in some meaningful way.
- Travel is your motivator. You want to spend a few months each year travelling in other countries.
- Perhaps paid employment is the funding source that allows you to put time into other pursuits that fulfil and energise you? Maybe you take classes, do volunteer work, polish your skills in sport or hobbies, build a part-time business in your discretionary time, are players or administrators in a favourite sport... the possibilities are immense.

There is no 'right' – only what is right for you. You might identify with

Mark Twain's quote: *The secret of success is making your vocation your vacation.*

Or perhaps Marsha Sinetar's definition is more apt for you. In *Do what you love, the money will follow* she says: *'Work is a way of being, an expression of love. A balanced person is always moving toward full participation in life, and growing in self-awareness, trust and high self-esteem. Abraham Maslow calls such healthy personalities 'self-actualizing', which means growing whole. They have taken moment-to-moment risks to ensure that their entire lives become an outward expression of their true inner selves. They have a sense of their own worth and are likely to experiment, to be creative, to ask for what they want and need. Their high self-esteem and subsequent risk-taking/creativity brings them skills that help them find the work they want, and to stick to their choices until financial rewards come. It is also often a slow and difficult path of self-discipline, perseverance and integrity.'*

Even if we fall into the work-loving category (and I'm one of them), we still need 'unwind' time.

BEWARE OF HURRY SICKNESS

'What is Hurry Sickness?' you may well ask. According to Chris Lewis in *Too fast to think: how to reclaim your creativity in a hyper-connected work culture* it is, *'A behaviour pattern characterized by continual rushing and anxiousness; an overwhelming and continual sense of urgency. A malaise in which a person feels chronically short of time and so tends to perform every task faster and to get flustered when encountering any kind of delay.'*

Dr Larry Dorsey describes it this way: *'It is expressed as heart disease, high blood pressure, or depression of our immune function, leading to an increased susceptibility to infection and cancer.'*

Neither sound much fun, yet hurry sickness is becoming more and more common. It will happen if we find ourselves so busy being busy that we feel ruled by time pressure instead of taking control of our time choices.

The average business person spends much of their day responding to external demands by colleagues, customers, and suppliers. Time to think, to analyse, to plan ahead? Sorry, can't fit it in right now. Parents have the same issue, especially when the children are young; there's never an end to the chores waiting attention. Many don't feel comfortable enjoying discretionary time until nothing obvious is waiting to be done (which is virtually never).

No-one can be totally active every minute of every day. Grant yourself permission to balance your day according to your values, needs and moods. It is your responsibility, no one else's, to make these choices. You cannot blame anyone else for lack of time – you are the person in charge of yourself.

WHAT STORY ARE YOU TELLING YOURSELF?

Most people plan their education and work, but not their leisure or how they want the overall picture of their life to be. And many think that if they work hard and reach certain achievements they will *then* be able to reward themselves. I'm not saying that's wrong, for there's a huge power in delayed gratification. *However*, when we start to think laterally about incorporating elements of long-term goals into our 'now' time, it is surprising what opportunities arise. You may wish to travel extensively overseas, but not be able to afford a long trip just now. What stops you from having a week or two of your annual leave out of your own country? These days it costs very little more to leave the country than to travel internally. Our minds, rather than reality, are the biggest blocks to new possibilities.

'Me' time is *not* selfish! If you've ever thought that giving yourself time out is selfish – *get over it!* In fact, it's a caring thing to do, for others as well as yourself. If you're burnt out and exhausted, who's going to do your job and keep your home fires brightly burning?

LONG HOURS – GOOD OR BAD?

Some corporate cultures encourage their employees to be 'married' to the job and a large number of senior executives are driven by the belief that the higher up the ladder they are, the longer the hours they have to do. Many self-employed people work well in excess of 60-70 hours per week. Others don't know any way to operate except by working extraordinarily long hours; their sense of identity is anchored in their work.

It's normal to work long hours when establishing a business or getting established in a new role. Successful people are very productive; none that I know have reached great success by working only 40 hours a week. So yes, for a time our lives are out of balance. However, as a long-term strategy it's a bad one. If a person's life is badly out of balance something will crack; eventually the relentless hours will cause them to lose what they've been striving for. Re-creation (work life balance) has to be planned for and scheduled in or it tends to slide unprotestingly away – for the moment.

Long hours do not necessarily equal effective hours.

One of my clients changed the culture of his company from *'we've got so much to do that we have to work long hours'* to *'we manage our load effectively and profitably within reasonable hours.'*

He was the owner of a very busy printing business and until two years before our conversation had regularly worked until about 8pm. They had a very intense workload. His staff of ten also worked similarly long hours.

Just before his first baby was due, he realised that if he was ever to see his child he needed to change his ways. He was also a keen sailor but frustrated with how seldom he got out on the water. Instead, his boat languished on the marina, growing weed and barnacles. It occurred to him that if he, the owner, was feeling hard-done-by and frustrated, his staff were almost certainly feeling the same.

With considerable anxiety about a possible loss of income, he decided to put a stop to the long hours.

'From now on we all leave the premises by 6pm, me included,' he announced to the team. *'It doesn't matter if we haven't finished the task we're working on. Unless it's life-threatening, leave it until tomorrow.'*

The result was startling. Not only did people get the same amount of work completed by 6pm that had previously taken up to two hours more per day, but the profitability of the firm increased. When they had less hours in which to get the work done, they were more focused and efficient instead of allowing the work to fill the time available. Also, because everyone had more free time they came into work rested and fresh.

If we eliminate as much as possible of the trivia in our lives, we create more hours to enjoy life, our families, our sports and other interests that a workaholic will say they are 'too busy' to pursue.

We cannot beat the Law of Balance; history abounds in examples of people who tried.

GUILT

What a useless emotion! The negative form of guilt is a close bed-fellow to the lack of self-esteem that sometimes prevents us from taking time for ourselves.

Do you sometimes feel unworthy to treat yourself to time out, perhaps because you think you don't 'deserve' a reward? It is often the state felt by people who tend to procrastinate on tasks and don't manage their time very well.

To overcome this feeling:

- Beat procrastination (see the previous chapter).
- Create and speak an affirmation such as: *'I deserve fun'* or *'I regularly make time for fun.'*
- Don't say *'I can't fit it in'*. Instead ask *'How can I fit it in?'* The quality of the question determines the quality of the answer.
- If you're getting stale on a project, take a short break with no guilt. It will enable you to return to the task much clearer and more effective. You have two choices, to feel good about a short stop, or guilty. Since rest is essential, learn to enjoy it.

ARE YOU HEADING IN THE RIGHT DIRECTION?

We often keep our nose to the grindstone, doing the work in front of us and getting the pay-rises (if we're lucky), without really regarding what we want out of life. What are your values? Are they congruent with your goals? What do you want to achieve, not just today, not just this week, but further out into the future?

How often do you *really* look around you? When did you last go for a walk or run in some beautiful natural setting? Have you been observing the changes of the seasons? How long is it since you just sat and observed the world around you?

Fleur discussed this values/goals issue with me over a 6-week period. It's often one of the hardest issues for people to get a grip on. She was a very hard-working wife and mother and, at that time, a salesperson. All her life she had been efficient – the sort who unintentionally makes a less-organised person feel inferior, simply because she packed a huge amount of activity into every day. Her passion, however, was the theatre.

Through our conversations she realised that her values – which revolved primarily round her wife, mother, theatre, and community service roles – didn't fit with her financial and work goals. The lack of congruence between, on one hand her work and financial goals, and on the other, her values, was causing an increasingly discomfort. Also, her awesome amount of activity didn't make her feel fulfilled as a person. Because she had such a happy home life she couldn't understand what was wrong. It seemed so ungrateful to be dissatisfied!

Although her income was useful to the family budget, it was possible for them to manage with less if necessary. We brainstormed lateral ideas regarding her income creation. It was only when she gave herself enough time to sit back and analyse her life that she suddenly saw what to do. By looking more closely at her core values, talking to me and others and expanding her thinking with reading and learning, she had opened her mind to other possibilities.

A few years later she had her own drama school for children. For a while she made less money, but that was never the issue anyway. She got her joy back; she was fulfilled by following her dream and making a difference in the lives of many youngsters. By carving a specialist niche in the drama field, she brought her values and her goals into alignment and achieved personal satisfaction.

EXERCISE:
- How many hours a week do you work? (Honestly!)
- Are you happy with that, or would you prefer to work less? Or more?
- What drives you?
- Do you have enough fun and regular 'relax' time with your family and friends?
- What tasks (that you're presently doing) could you delegate or eliminate?
- How often do you push your weary body, when every muscle and fibre screams 'stop'?
- When did you last slow down to think, and write, about the 'big' issues of life – how you want your life to be and whether your activities are congruent with your values?
- When did you last take an hour (or more) to forward plan?
- When you last took some planning time, how did you feel?
- What fun activities are you currently telling yourself you haven't got time to do?
- Are you sure about that? Spend some time thinking outside the box about other ways of creating time for recreation. Don't stop until you've come up with at least three alternatives.
- Who has an interest in helping you get a better life balance?
- At what times of day are you most productive?
- Write down your own personal affirmations about quality of life.

A SMORGASBORD OF STRATEGIES

CREATIVE PROCRASTINATION
One of the strategies that helps with our work life balance is what I also call creative procrastination. I love explaining – it's like telling people

that sometimes chocolate and ice-cream are actually good for you! You thought procrastination was a naughty word, didn't you? You're only partly right. There are times when procrastination is the right choice of action. To know when and what to delay on – that's the art of creating balance and effectiveness in our lives.

As we discussed in the previous chapter, negative procrastination is putting off until tomorrow that which should be done today. On the other hand, creative procrastination is good. It is deliberate – planning and scheduling time for your own use. It is also choosing to procrastinate on Reactive activities with their Frenetic flags waving, so you can work on long-term Proactive actions, including time out or activities that re-energise you.

My definition of creative procrastination is:

> *Putting off until tomorrow that which won't advance your life plan by being done today.*
> *It is also the planned and deliberate gift of prime time to yourself regularly, doing what gives you greatest satisfaction, including not doing anything, if that's your choice.*
>
> *It is learning how to leave undone those things which didn't really need to be done, so that you achieve balance and satisfaction in your life.*

We've been brought up to regard 'doing nothing' as bad. Is it? How about adopting a new paradigm about 'think' and 'play' time?

'Sometimes we simply need to unlearn our polarized belief that only work is important and realize that without refreshing, renewing play, we lower our capacity for high-quality work and our ability to enjoy life fully.' Ann McGee-Cooper.

We've talked about energy management rather than just time management. To achieve that, we must pay attention to health, relaxation and creativity, stress reduction and sheer joy of living – having fun!

Creative procrastination is one of the answers!

UTILISE THE 80/20 RULE

How does the 80/20 rule apply in creative procrastination?

Learn to focus on the activities that make a difference. Whatever you pay attention to, you will be good at. Focus on negative influences in your life and you will be excellently negative; focus on 'busy work' and you'll be excellent on detail and trivia; focus on the major task or tasks that are going to propel you to new levels of achievement and you'll reach those new levels and beyond. As you exclude or procrastinate on the things that do not matter and spend time on meaningful projects and people, over time you'll dramatically improve your quality of life.

It takes practise to be comfortable with this balance but if you keep attending to the top priority activities every day in all the ways we've discussed, one day, I promise you, you'll find that trivia is not taking as much of your time.

LISTEN TO YOUR BODY

It's common to ignore the messages our bodies try to give us and keep working even when ill or exhausted; we're conditioned to using our time 'fully'. I've ignored those messages myself but guess what – I never win an argument with my body! Pushing yourself in this way simply leads to stress, illness and inefficiency.

The owner of a day-care centre had just had a staff member leave, causing her to work longer shifts each day. She was so tired that she couldn't see that 'more hours' did not equal 'more productivity'. She was starting her days feeling tired; pushing herself to do everything she thought she 'ought' to do and not delegating tasks to others because she didn't want to be 'unfair'. Each day she got less and less done and felt more and more exhausted. She wondered why she had a cold and felt guilty about all manner of things that weren't flowing well.

I encouraged her to go home for a sleep and find someone to take charge so she could have the next day off. She reported back a few days later that the time off changed everything. Staff filled the gaps, problems didn't seem so bad any more and she learned that it was fine to give herself permission to stop when the body demanded it.

Don't feel guilty about stopping when you're exhausted.

PLAN YOUR PLAY TIME

If you plan your recreational time as carefully as you do your business activities, it's surprising how many special and memorable events can be fitted into your life.

Sometimes people look at me in horror when I suggest that they set aside special time for their loved ones. One man reported that his partner become quite annoyed at being treated as a 'scheduled item'. But – when I asked how long it had been since their last date night, he couldn't recall.

How much do you remember of the last month's unscheduled 'go with the flow' activities with your loved ones? Do any wonderful enriching highlights jump out at you from last week's TV viewing together? On the other hand, think about the last time you arranged a special outing. How much detail comes to mind? Who did you see? What was the day like? What did you eat, and where? In this area, as with everything else in the way we use our lives, planning is king. It isn't restrictive – it's liberating and enriching. It actually allows more flexibility.

How often have you heard people say *'When I've got visitors I see local places I would otherwise ignore'*? I've certainly fallen into that trap!

Many years ago I lived at Ninety Mile Beach, in the Far North of New Zealand. My home was very close to the water. Sure enough, I found that after about six months I started to take it for granted. Fortunately for my memory bank, in the last year I made a new friend. Rose, who lived in the nearby town, loved the beach with a passion. Why she hadn't bought at the beach I'll never know, because every possible weekend she would jump in her car and come out. Often she would turn up at my place and say, *'Come on, Robyn. Let's go down to the beach'*. I'd be engrossed in absolutely exciting (not!) activities like housework, ironing or gardening and have to make a conscious effort of will to shift my head on to recreation. The funny thing is – I don't remember the uncompleted housework ever being a major problem. The kids still got fed and the house was seldom a complete tip. What I do still remember, even years later, are many wonderful summer days on the beach with Rose.

This idea of scheduling in your family and recreational activities may seem very alien. You may have to make quite major lifestyle changes. But I encourage you to give it a go.

MICRO BREAKS (short pauses through the day)

Because Sanity Gaps are part of my message, I almost always ask my audiences if they take a regular lunch break and how many take tea breaks – not just the 'grab a cuppa and take it back to the desk' kind of tea break, but a real one where they give their brain a rest, away from their desk.

Typically, more than 70 percent of the room don't do either on a regular basis. The next questions are *'how effective are you in the afternoon?'* and *'how tired are you at the end of the day?'* Those who don't take breaks, almost without exception, admit to a major energy slump and often exhaustion by knock-off time. By end of day they drag their weary bodies home – not much use to themselves or the loving families waiting for their share of time. As we discuss it, the look on their faces is classic – a kind of bemused *'why didn't I notice that connection before?'*

Various biological rhythms flow through our body all day, all night. Ultradian rhythms are some of them. Loosely translated, 'ultra' means 'many' and 'dian' means 'day' – the many rhythms of the day. They cycle continuously through our body like rolling waves – 90-120 minutes in the upper cycle, 15-20 minutes in the dip – repeated day and night.

The dip cycle is not a negative thing. Instead, it's the rest cycle that our body needs in order to recharge, rebuild and grow. If we keep pushing through, if we don't give our body a chance to recharge, we push the poor old thing into flight or fight.

The consequence? Stress, burnout, and eventually sickness – sometimes very severe and long-lasting.

So, what to do about it? Morning and afternoon tea breaks and a lunch break away from your desk – they're some of the simple solutions. And what about Winston Churchill's technique – the one that kept him operating at full steam through all those tough war years? He was famous for his power naps. When tired he'd pop upstairs (when he was working at Downing

Street) and hop into bed for about 20 minutes. He also had a special nap chair near his office. Other significant historical people who applied the same technique: Margaret Thatcher, John F. Kennedy, Beethoven, Benjamin Franklin, Leonardo Da Vinci, Eleanor Roosevelt, Brahms, John D. Rockefeller, Dali, Robert Louis Stevenson and Albert Einstein. And there are many modern well-known people with the same technique.

'But I work in a corporate environment and can't take a nap', you might be saying. There's ample evidence to show that taking a short break during your work day will pay dividends in productivity, reduces mistakes and is great for your well-being. If you take the time to notice the messages your body sends, and if you can show your employer or colleagues the benefits they reap from your increased effectiveness in the afternoon, you might be surprised how much support you get. It's not uncommon in some countries, including China, to see people napping at their desks after lunch. And what about the famous continental siesta?

A young accountant in a large city office in New Zealand, with full knowledge of his colleagues, often took a 20-minute nap at his desk in the early afternoon. If he was really tired he'd shut the door (he was lucky enough to have one!) and lie down on the floor. When he surfaced again he'd sometimes feel a little dozy for a couple of minutes but then his renewed energy would kick in. He operated at far higher efficiency for the rest of the day than if he'd tried to push through the exhaustion zone.

Maybe you don't have the luxury of a door. Other solutions include driving your car at lunchtime to a nearby park. When I was a young woman and recovering from glandular fever, in summer I often walked to the nearby park and dozed under a tree. Maybe you can use a sick room. And quiet rooms are now in vogue. Firms such Unilever, Google, Ben and Jerry's, Zappos, Nike, Huffington Post and NASA (and that's just for starters) provide dedicated rooms or sleep pods for meditation, prayer, quiet relaxation or napping – no talking allowed.

Signs that you need an Ultradian break, a micro break, a siesta, a meditation break, a power nap, a NASA nap (whichever name works for you): Tiredness, yawning, irritability, mistakes (very obvious when you're at a keyboard), thirsty, unfocused and sometimes aching body parts – often the back or shoulders.

MACRO BREAKS (about every six weeks)

Stress is an insidious creeping problem. It sneaks up on us without our being aware of it and next thing, we're sick. However, we can keep it under control if we regularly have what I call macro breaks.

The purpose of this was explained to me by a nutritionist many years ago: *'If you think of all the stressors in your life as individual stress bricks, every time you experience a stressful situation, or are particularly busy, you're building a stress wall around yourself. If you just keep going, the wall has nowhere to go but up. When people who live this way finally take a holiday they spend the first week being exhausted and usually sick.*

'The best way to keep the stress wall at a healthy level is to take a break of a few days about every six weeks. This knocks some of the bricks down and keeps the wall always at a manageable height.'

I like to think of these weekend breaks as 'spontaneous time' or 'do nothing' weekends.

Two applications:

An early-childhood teacher with a family found the weekends were even busier than the weeks. Each of the four children played sport. She and her husband decided to schedule a 'free weekend' about every six weeks. Anything that needed doing before the beginning of the following week (such as groceries, washing or housework) was handled on the Thursday night. Then, on Friday night after they'd all arrived home from work or school they went into 'spontaneous time'.

Sometimes they'd stay home and just chill out – no work, no duties or obligations. Other times they'd get in the car and just drive, stopping when they felt like it and staying overnight if they wanted to. It was a wonderfully rejuvenating experience and so valuable that even after the children left home, she and her husband continued the same pattern.

A young working mother in the medical field had a clever variation.

She and her family didn't have spare cash for weekends away, but they recognised the value of 'time off'. About every six weeks they told their friends and extended family they were going away but – they stayed home. They shut the gate, pulled down the curtains at the front of the house, turned the phones off and just relaxed. The children had a back yard to play in; the parents kicked back. The only rule was: *no work*. She reported the same benefits as the teacher.

If you're able to extend some of those breaks to three or four days, you'll get even more value. It's highly unlikely that you'll then come down ill when you take your annual holidays.

BLOCK IN 'TIME OUT' – EVERY WEEK

Recharge and personal time is too important to leave to chance – it needs to be planned for. If you've started consistently planning your week rather than just your day, as we've already discussed, it's far easier to schedule 'me' time. Instead of squeezing personal activities into gaps in your diary, schedule 'recharge time' as a priority and fit other activities around it.

SEPARATE HOME AND BUSINESS

This is one of the hardest issues for many, and even more challenging if you work with family members. Trouble is, keeping going becomes a habit. Decide on an action that says 'we're done for the day'. It might be turning off the computer, shutting the home office door or a humorous penalty system (like a Fines Jar) if work is discussed after a set time.

A FINAL SMORGASBORD OF 'CHILL OUT' SUGGESTIONS:
- Drive home by a lovely setting and stop for ten minutes to walk in the fresh air.
- Give yourself permission to play. Ask yourself, *'If I give myself 30 minutes a day to do anything I like, what would I do and when and where would I do it?'* Just the very idea of regular 'me' time is energising and exciting (and for some it's so uncommon that at first it's scary!) If you're in a family or partnership, you can support each other to have this space. It might be that you get up

30 minutes earlier than the family and use it as your quiet time.

- Change your clothes and take a shower as soon as you walk in from work – cast off the day's events by casting off the clothes.
- Instead of turning on the TV with its attendant crop of noise and disasters, put on some quiet relaxing music.
- Get into a regular exercise programme. If you don't like exercising alone, find a support group or start one.
- Have a regular time to stop. Many people have a ritual 'before-dinner' drink where they sit down and relax. If possible, avoid having such a break with the 6 o'clock news – instead of relaxing you're bringing in the world. No 'me time' there – just gloom and doom!
- Don't do email after a certain time at night, say 7 or 8pm. If you don't set a regular switch-off time you'll go to bed with work issues still rolling round your brain. That then affects the quality of your sleep.

KEY POINT No. 33: *Sanity gaps are too important to leave to chance. Schedule them.*

CONCLUSION

I wish you well, as I wave you goodbye

So you want the bottom line on taking control of your life? Perhaps you see people around you making great strides forward, but so far success seems to be just beyond your grasp? You ask yourself if you're doing the right things to reach your goals. You've been studying about how to use your time better, you've got the theory base, you've got the practical specifics, so how can you capitalise on your new knowledge and make sure you get where you want to go?

You've got it in your grasp. There is no mystique about it – success comes one small step at a time. Every person who achieves their goals in life is very focused on the way they use their time. They have a strong sense that their time is precious and irreplaceable. Don't squander it.

What is success to you? What gives you greatest personal satisfaction? Are you prepared to commit to building improved habits? Have you developed the long view? Every extraordinary achievement in human life is the result of thousands of ordinary efforts that are seldom seen or appreciated.

DISCIPLINE

All through this book we've talked about developing self-discipline to prioritise our daily activities. Not a rigid, life-quenching discipline, however, but a method that allows us freedom and flexibility.

By daily doing the most vital and important activities, and including Proactive activities as often as possible, you *will* reach your goals, whatever they may be. Become result-oriented, not action-oriented. Recognise that this means focusing as many of your actions as possible on the long-term. Don't let your days be gobbled up with undirected or low-value activities – develop or expand your focus and purpose.

And, at the same time, keep some balance in your life. Don't ignore your family, friends, and health in a mad scramble towards your goals or you may be very lonely, sick and tired when you've achieved them.

Be courageous. Take risks. Step out into the unknown. People who play safe and never test their boundaries remain comfortably in their ruts. What is the difference between a rut and a grave? With a rut you have a choice to step out; with a grave, you don't!

Don't accept other people's judgments of you. Believe in yourself and don't focus on your present circumstances. Even when you're not sure where you're going and the path is not clear, keep believing in yourself and your ability to get out of the mud. I've lived the principles and techniques I talk about in this book and, dear reader, they work. They're road-tested and will put you on the highway to whatever success you choose, if you're prepared to do the small unsung steps, day after day.

People who develop a long view and make decisions accordingly are the achievers of life. Success comes in the moments when no-one else is looking. It's the accumulation of a lifetime of little actions. If you doubt me, do your own survey of people whom you consider to be successful. Whatever their chosen path in life, they will have all sacrificed something to reach their present position. We earn what we deserve. I know it's a cliché, but there are no free lunches in life. Nor do well-integrated families and loving relationships happen by themselves. Good fortune is earned, not given!

I'd like to leave you with some of my favourite inspirational quotes.

From Napoleon Hill: *'There are no limitations to the mind, except those we acknowledge.'*

From Anita Roddick, the inspirational founder of Body Shop and a great humanitarian: *'I think the older you get the more you realise that this is no dress rehearsal, so you feel you want to put more into life. I am always astonished and grateful, when I wake up in the morning, to be alive. The thought that every day might be my last, and the desire to make the most of every moment, drives me on.'* Sadly, she died far too young – only 64 – which makes her words all the more poignant.

And finally, from George Bernard Shaw: *'This is the true joy in life . . . being used for a purpose recognised by yourself as a mighty one . . . being a force of Nature instead of a feverish selfish little clod of ailments and grievances complaining that the world will not devote itself to making you happy . . . I am of the opinion that my life belongs to the whole community and as long as I live it is my privilege to do for it whatever I can.*

'I want to be thoroughly used up when I die. For the harder I work the more I live. I rejoice in life for its own sake. Life is no brief candle to me. It's a sort of splendid torch which I've got to hold up for the moment and I want to make it burn as brightly as possible before handing it on to future generations.'

Success is not an accident — it's a decision. Make it happen, and have a great life.

Are you ready for further support?

If you've not yet done it, your **free** audio downloads wait for you at http://gettingagrip.com/digitalgifts.

When you register to get your downloads you'll also receive a well-spaced supply of ongoing time tips and practical help. Should you wish to unsubscribe at any time, it's as easy as one click. We don't spam you and never share your details.

SOURCES AND FURTHER READING

Bach, Richard. *Illusions: The Adventures of a Reluctant Messiah*. Pan Books. 1977, 2001.

Blanchard, Kenneth, Oncken, William, Jr., and Burrows, Hal. *The One Minute Manager Meets the Monkey*. Fontana, 1999, 2011.

Blanchard, Kenneth, Zigarmi, Patricia and Zigarmi, Drea. *Leadership and the One Minute Manager*. William Morrow. 1st ed. 1985, Updated 1999.

Canfield, Jack, and Hansen, Mark Victor. *Chicken Soup for the Soul*. Health Communications, 1993, 2013.

Chin, Paul. http://www.paulchinonline.com

Cleese, John. *Meetings, Bloody Meetings*. Video Arts training video, 1974.

Covey, Stephen R. *7 Habits of Highly Effective People*. Simon & Schuster, 1989, 2013.

de Bono, Edward. *Six Thinking Hats*. MICA Management Resources, 1985, rev. & updated 1999.

Dossey, Larry. *Space, Time and Medicine*. Shambhala Publications, Random House, 1982.

Douglass, Merrill E. and Douglass, Donna N. *Manage Your Time, Your Work, Yourself*. AMACOM, 1980, updated 1993.

Drucker, Peter F. *The Effective Executive*. HarperCollins, 1967, multiple reprints, 2006.

Franklin, Benjamin. *The Autobiography of Benjamin Franklin*. (with an introduction by Henry Ketcham), Digireads.com Publishing, 2016. First published 1789.

Gawain, Shakti. *Creative Visualization*. New World Library, 1978, 1995, 2002.

Gerber, Michael E. *The E-Myth Revisited: Why Most Small Businesses Don't Work and What to do About It*. HarperCollins, 2001.

Hill, Napoleon. *Law of Success*. Orne Publishing, 2010. First published 1925.

Hill, Napoleon. *Think and Grow Rich*. Napoleon Hill Foundation, 2016. First published 1937.

Hill, Napoleon. *The Master-Key to Riches*. Napoleon Hill Foundation, 2018. First published 1945.

Hunt, Des. *What Makes People Tick: How to Understand Yourself and Others*. AWC Business Solutions, 1988, updated and revised 2014.

Kehoe, John. *Mind Power into the 21ˢᵗ Century*. 1997, Zoetic, 2011.

Lewis, Chris. *Too Fast to Think: how to reclaim your creativity in a hyper-connected work culture*. Kogan Page, 2016.

Lewis, David. *Mindlab International*. https://www.youtube.com/watch?v=qWlw1Kga_1A and reported by Lauren Davidson in The Telegraph 2 June, 2016.

McGee-Cooper, Ann, and Trammell, Duane. *Time Management for Unmanageable People*. Bantam, 1994.

Pearce, Robyn. *Getting A Grip on Life Goals Toolkit*. https://www.gettingagrip.com/product/getting-a-grip-on-life-goals-toolkit/

Pearce, Robyn. *Getting a Grip on Planning and Prioritising Online Study Course*. https://www.gettingagrip.com/product/getting-a-grip-on-planning-and-prioritising-4-part-course/

Perlow, Leslie A, Hadley, Constance Noonan & Eun, Eunice. *Stop the meeting madness*. Harvard Business Review. July/August 2017.

Roddick, Anita. *Body & Soul*. Ebury Press, 1991.

Sigman, Aric. *Remotely Controlled: How television is damaging our lives*. Vermilion, 2007.

Sigman, Aric. *Time For a View on Screen Time*. Archives of Disease in Childhood. British Medical Journals, Nov 2012. Vol 97 Issue 11:935 – 942.

Sigman, Aric. *Visual voodoo: the biological impact of watching TV*. Article published in Biologist, Feb 2007 Vol 54:1.

Sinetar, Marsha. *Do What You Love, The Money Will Follow*. Dell, 1987. Sinetar & Ass, 2015.

Snooks, Steuart. *The 7 Critical Impacts of Information & E-mail Overload* – free download. https://www.steuartsnooks.com.au/resources/

Song, Mike. *Get Control.* http://www.getcontrol.net/ (Survey on usage of paper diaries)

Spira, Jonathan. *Overload! How Too Much Information Is Hazardous To Your Organization.* Wiley, 2011.

Tracy, Brian. *Master Your Time, Master Your Life.* Random, 2017.

Tracy, Brian. *Maximum Achievement: strategies and skills that will unlock your hidden powers to succeed.* Simon & Schuster, 1993, 1995.

Twain, Mark. *The Adventures of Tom Sawyer.* Dover Publications, 1998. First published 1876.

University of Illinois at Urbana-Champaign. *Happiness Improves Health and Lengthens Life.* Science Daily, March 1, 2011.

Wilde, Stuart. *Life Was Never Meant to be a Struggle.* Hay House, 1987.

About Time: 120 Tips for Those with No Time

Have you ever thought: *'There must be a quicker way?'*

Are you challenged by too many time choices, too much to do, but don't have enough hours in the day?

This book is a 'quick-dip' of tried and true practical tips from real people – tips that will help you find those missing hours.

Tips include how to:

Robyn Pearce

ABOUT TIME
120 time-saving
tips for those
with no time

3rd EDITION

- Overcome procrastination
- Work more effectively with others
- Manage your computer efficiently
- Get back your life, even if you work from home
- Turn meetings from time-wasters to time-savers
- Handle paper and information more efficiently
- And much, much more ....

'I keep **About Time** *in my car and dip in whenever I'm waiting for my kids. Pure gold.'* Susannah Bernstein, lawyer and mother.

'While fixing a computer for a colleague I noticed your book, started perusing, and then borrowed it. Can't wait to try some of the ideas!' Debbie Webb, IT Helpdesk Supervisor.

'Sensible and easy to manage tips on time management, well presented in no nonsense words. Robyn feels like a friend ...yet we have never met.' Sally Wang, Malaysia.

'Fantastic hints which I have used as a health promoter across all life spans'. Lyn Burns.

Purchase now at https://www.gettingagrip.com/products/ebooks/

Getting a Grip on the Paper & Information War

How often do you stop at your desk, look at the teetering piles of paper, and either threaten arson or feel like hiding? The 'paper and information war' is fought by millions of people every day – and *you* can win it!

Robyn Pearce's no-nonsense advice will give you:

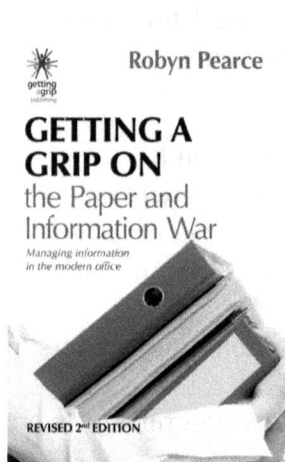

Robyn Pearce

GETTING A GRIP ON
the Paper and
Information War

Managing information
in the modern office

REVISED 2ⁿᵈ EDITION

- Fast easy ways to handle paper & electronic information
- Increased productivity and *much* less stress
- The most efficient filing systems for *you*
- Less clutter screaming *'Deal with me now!'*
- Fast reading and reduced reading piles
- An efficient home office
- ... and much more

'I feel like I've been given the keys to a large end V8 after sitting in a trumped-up shopping trolley waiting for the lights to turn green...' Phil Mitchell, Insurance Officer.

'The light has gone on! It isn't rocket science, but until you read a logical step-by-step book like this, the obvious isn't obvious. My desk has never been so tidy and work so up to date, even at the end of the month.' Gail Leighton, Office Manager, Accounting Firm.

'I started reading Getting a Grip on the Paper War on a flight from London to a book fair in Prague. I'd only intended to have a quick scan. But you hooked me in! I grabbed paper from my bag and began to take notes. When I ran out of paper I scribbled all over the paper bag provided by the airline (won't mention what it's normally used for!). Once I reached the hotel, instead of going out to eat I stayed in my room, kept on reading and taking notes. I love the way you showed me simple ways to sort and manage the crap all over my desk.' Anita, Publisher's Foreign Rights Rep.

Purchase now at https://www.gettingagrip.com/products/ebooks/

Getting a Grip on Parenting Time

In this easy-to-read, light-hearted and practical book you'll find 86 time-saving parenting tips and tricks as well as heart-warming encouragement for confused, overloaded and time-poor parents who wonder if they're doing this parenting gig right.

Enjoy and learn from the Time Queen Robyn Pearce, mother of six, grandmother of seventeen and international time and productivity specialist.

Tips on:

Robyn Pearce

GETTING A GRIP ON
Parenting Time
86 Commonsense Lessons From The Trenches

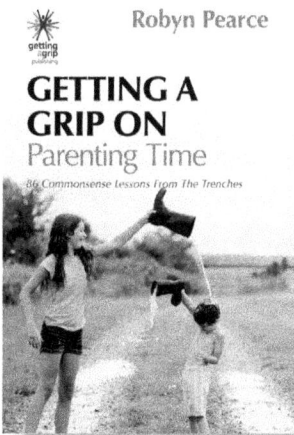

- How to get the kids to help around the house
- Making time for each child
- Coping with technology
- Fast *and* healthy food – yes, you can have both!
- Getting teenagers to take responsibility
- How parents can still have a life!
- Time-saving housework tips
- Think like a nanny – and get the chores done earlier
- And heaps more ...

This book is Robyn's finest work to date. She has cleverly combined her professional acumen with her experience of life to produce this wonderfully practical parenting handbook. **Yvonne Godfrey,** Founder of MIOMO (Making It On My Own) & host parent on reality TV show, The World's Strictest Parents.

'Parents have so much information and advice to wade through, that to hear from a wise, sensible, funny and practical Mum and Grandma like Robyn, is very refreshing and helpful. Parents will pick up her book and find themselves nodding, feeling encouraged and empowered to make little and significant changes. This book offers interesting and practical tips from start to finish and includes current research.

'Robyn is "passing the baton on" in this wonderful book – her thoughts and reflections make absolute sense, are good for families and relationships and can be used in any family, no matter what size or shape.' **Jenny Hale,** The Parenting Place.

'What a heap of wonderful and VERY practical observations, suggestions and useful advice, supported by research, to guide even the most confused parent and every family, regardless of age and stage of children, (even for grannies!).' **Anna Ryan**, Ryan Publications.

Purchase now at https://amzn.to/2Q3K9Qf

Getting a Grip on Leadership:
How to learn leadership without making all the mistakes yourself

by Robyn Pearce and LaVonn Steiner

Leadership specialist LaVonn Steiner (USA) and multi-title time management expert Robyn Pearce (New Zealand) bring you lessons learned the hard way, starting from little or no leadership experience.

No time is wasted on academic theories with limited real-world relevance. Instead, they focus on real-life techniques and examples you can use immediately.

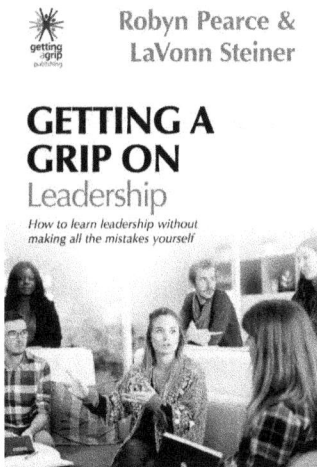

Robyn Pearce &
LaVonn Steiner

GETTING A GRIP ON
Leadership
How to learn leadership without making all the mistakes yourself

- If you struggle with leadership of your team ...
- Or you're caught up in power struggles or turf battles...
- Some of your team are fearful of new challenges...
- Perhaps you're a perfectionist and hate passing the work to someone else ...
- Giving negative feedback is highly uncomfortable ...
- Maybe you're feeling overwhelmed and out of control ...
- You're desperate for some easy planning and project tools ...
- And you're searching for more peace at work and home

With the practical steps and examples in this book you'll learn simple methods to turn your problem staff into high-functioning teams. And you'll be a more effective leader.

'Required reading for everyone ... clear, practical, and easy to read ... gives readers guidance on actual implementation... Section on strategic planning with tracking tools the best I've seen.' Linda Knodel, Snr VP/

Chief Nursing Officer, St. Alexius Medical Center, Bismarck ND.

' ..*romped through your book in 8 days ... intend to refer to it many times in the future. The many concepts and ideas will certainly help me become a better manager.*' Steve Wangler, Snr VP, Bank Center First, North Dakota.

'*I am not a reader but I am obsessed with reading this book. I was writing like a mad-man, taking lots of notes!*' Melanie Marquart, Marketing Processing and Executive Assistant, SIA – Schmidt Insurance providing services for 8000 agents in 30 US states

'*Getting a grip on Leadership is very good. It's had a major impact on me. I realised I'd lost my way a bit re who I am. Have done the exercises and am finding me. It's actually been a long time! Thanks so much and congratulations to you and LaVonn.*' Heather Millar, Manager, Professional Practise, Central North Island Kindergarten Association, New Zealand

Purchase now at https://www.gettingagrip.com/products/ebooks/

About Time for Teaching:
120 time-saving tips for teachers and those who support them

Teachers and administrators in several countries share their 'best practise' ideas, interwoven with Robyn Pearce's delightful and relaxed time management wisdom.

Robyn Pearce

getting
agrip
publishing

ABOUT TIME
for Teaching
120 time-saving tips for teachers and those
who support them

- Stop the clutter of unwanted material
- Reduce interruptions
- Leave problems where they belong
- Have a life outside of school
- Enjoy your own kids, even after a hard day at school
- Hire the best staff
- Simplify and reduce meetings
- Get information back from others on time
- Educate over-enthusiastic board members
- Use technology to save time
- Find and use volunteers effectively
- Reduce panic and stress in unexpected situations
- ... plus four chapters on efficiency tips for the school office

'Follow Robyn's advice. It makes a difference.' Owen Hoskin, Past Principal, Henderson High, New Zealand

Purchase now at https://www.gettingagrip.com/products/ebooks/

ABOUT THE AUTHOR

Robyn Pearce has learnt her skills and knowledge about time management and productivity from the ground up. In fact, she's made just about all the mistakes you could imagine – and survived!

From humble beginnings as a farmer's wife, mother of six (including an intellectually handicapped foster son), then a solo mother and real estate agent, Robyn had to learn better time management skills – or sink!

However, once she started to focus on improvement, she turned her biggest weakness into a major strength. Since 1992, as a keynote speaker, trainer and author she has shared her experiences and knowledge with thousands of clients in many industries around the world, helping them win their time battles. As a speaker she holds the top accreditation of CSP (Certified Speaking Professional), held by less than 1% of professional speakers worldwide.

She's a prolific author, regular columnist and contributor to many journals and the New Zealand Herald online and expert commentator for radio, television and online blogs.

At the GettingAGrip.com website you'll find all manner of further resources to assist you in your time-learning journey. Be sure to request your free report 'How to Master Time in Only 90 Seconds' at www. gettingagrip.com

And remember to grab your five **free** audio downloads at http://gettingagrip.com/digitalgifts on how to make time for exercise, how to control your Inbox, practical advice on goals, simplicity, managing major projects and more.

www.ingramcontent.com/pod-product-compliance
Lightning Source LLC
Chambersburg PA
CBHW070716220326
41598CB00024BA/3185